Tears of Joy
and
Tears of Sorrow

Tears of Joy
and
Tears of Sorrow

A Guidebook about the Meaning,
Make-up, and Conduct of a Wedding and a
Funeral for Theological Students, Pastors,
and Worship Committee Members

by

Warren C. Brannon, Sr.

VANTAGE PRESS
New York

Cover design by Susan Thomas

FIRST EDITION

Published by Vantage Press, Inc.
419 Park Ave. South, New York, NY 10016

Manufactured in the United States of America
ISBN: 0-533-15203-8

Library of Congress Catalog Card No.: 2005902462

0 9 8 7 6 5 4 3 2 1

Contents

Preface

As any pastor who has been out of the chute a time or two will readily tell you, on the occasions of funerals AND weddings, *there shall be tears* ... TEARS OF JOY and TEARS OF SORROW. Many of these flowing displays of emotion often derive from the confusion and conflicts that arise between those leading these services and those on whose behalf they are planned. The pastor may discover as either big occasion nears that not everyone naturally agrees about what should take place at a wedding or a funeral. It is imperative that we clergy first clarify our own understanding of what in the name of Christ we are about in celebration of these two occasions. With this little book I hope to contribute to this process.

Wedding and funeral services generally come under the category of things about which busy pastors say, "If it ain't broke, don't dare even try to fix it!" When each celebration arises, the easiest thing to do is simply to reach for our trusty book of printed generic services and read, unabridged, from its pages. Such services would be just as much at home in the hallowed halls of the courthouse as in the sacred sanctuaries of the church house. There is an urgent need for worship leaders and pastors to supply proper guidance and support to our people, to focus some quality thought on weddings and funerals so that they will accurately reflect the sound principles of the Christian faith, Christian worship and solid pastoral experience. I have no desire to portray all of these special services of the Church as being identical. I do, however, advocate that they be presented in the form of a service of worship, which is too often not the case in the churches of today.

On the occasions of weddings and funerals, our people come to the Church for help in planning something that is beyond the bounds of their ordinary experience. This offers the Church an opportunity to give them what they intuitively seek, since we possess the appropriate training and experience to do so. In so doing, we pastors should rediscover our capacity for creating rites that are relevant, personal, and immensely satisfying to all concerned, avoiding the "sweet," "cute" collage of sights and sounds often witnessed in the worldly society of which we are a part.

Much of the material in this book is duplicated in various other places. I have tried to draw it all together here and detail what to do and how to do it and what it all means. A pastoral guide for pastors, if you will. Included in these pages are such rare literary jewels as the job description for the wedding director and the breakdown and history of the two rites involved in the conventional wedding service. They will most certainly help shape your way of conducting the marriage rites.

My prayer is that my fifty-year pastoral experience has garnered pearls of great price in the form of thought-provoking ideas that will contribute to your deeper understanding of both weddings and funerals, with the result that these special worship services will reflect more distinctly the essence of the Christian faith in action.

W.C.B.

Tears of Joy
and
Tears of Sorrow

PART ONE

The Introduction

1

The Nature of Wedding and Funeral Services

Are They Ordinances of the Church . . . or Tribal Tattoos?

We embark on the examination of wedding and funeral services by striving to arrive at some basic agreement about exactly who is in charge of their make-up. Who has the say-so about which elements of worship are rightly and necessarily to be included in a wedding or a funeral service? Is it proper for anybody (or everybody) to piece together special services like these? We may just as well be asking a question like, "Who decides what is good grammar?"

Oftentimes such important matters as these are not explored in detail in theological schools. Students there are generally expected to pick them up along the way. Unfortunately, some folks who hack out the paths of experience before us lead us astray. Worship leaders do precious little study of weddings and funerals and display a dismal degree of understanding them. And this is a shame, partly because these are occasions when the beliefs and practices of the Christian faith are very much on public display. When the occasions for their use arise, we simply reach for the appropriate printed service and read from its pages unabridged. Hopefully, you will shortly discover the need to adapt these services into the forms of worship they are meant to be. Something is broken, and we can jolly well fix it!

Monica, a young bride-to-be, and her mother march into the pastor's office one morning to engage in the initial planning session for the young lady's wedding, which they hope to schedule in the sanctuary a few months hence. No sooner have the ladies settled onto the couch there when the mother pulls out a sheet of paper and begins to read a detailed description of what she and the bride want the wedding service to be like—including what members of the wedding party are to wear, where they are to be positioned, what music is to be played and sung, where the minister is to stand and what he is to wear and say, etc. It is all right there on that piece of paper.

They showed up for this first wedding planning session having already done all of the planning! What are they doing there, anyway?

What they are actually there to do is to "hire the hall" and to engage the services of the pastor to perform the wedding service just as they had it laid out. In their rationale, since they are producing the wedding and paying the bills for it, they thus have every right to expect everything to be done as they have designed, without regard for the meaning of the service or the customs of the Church.

Are they right or wrong? To whom does the wedding service belong?

Switch scenes! It is the end of a hard day for a family in the halls of a hospital. The pastor is there trying to help the new widow and the rest of her family maintain some kind of control after the man of the house has died during a seemingly simple operation. His sudden death has immediately immersed them into more desperate thoughts and emotions than those with which anybody could normally deal. Urging them on beyond where they now are or need to be, the pastor mentions more than once during the heavy evening, "The funeral service will be just exactly what the family says they want it to be. You all watch and see if that is not the way it will be."

Under the guise of being very open and considerate of the family's feelings, the pastor, who has conducted a large number of funeral services over the years, in reality appears to be dumping the responsibility for organizing this funeral on the family, none of whom has ever planned a funeral and possibly had not even attended one. They are all grappling with an incredible complex of issues in the advent of this completely unforeseen death, and now comes the summons for them to compose themselves and take charge of the design of the funeral service. All the while, however, through their demeanor, they have been screaming out to the pastor, "Tell us the appropriate things to do. What do people customarily do in such a situation as this? We don't have a clue! We desperately need your guidance and advice."

Perhaps the pastor is thinking that if the people have any criticism of the funeral service later on, he will not be the one to blame. A less than noble motive! He is obviously not thinking of what he is equipped to teach and to give in the name of the Body of Christ.

So it goes with any pastor. He or she is often faced with helping to put into good order the rites that signal both the beginning of married life and those marking the end of life itself.

Both of the above stories are authentic.

Like it or not, such duties as these are an integral part of a person's call to be a parish pastor. A pastor has both the training in these matters and the experience that yield the substance of sound guidance to share with the people when the needs arise. No wonder that it is true: There shall be tears of joy and tears of sorrow.

Friends, these two little scenarios indicate some very basic things that need to be established very early on in our deliberations about weddings and funerals. We're talking here about two well-established ordinances of the Church. When these rites are needed, people actually have certain options about where to turn for guidance and support: to the Church, to the clerk of court on the occasion of marriage, or to some fraternal organization in the case of the last rites.

When they turn to the Church at the time that a wedding is at hand, they do so for a profound reason which may escape even them at the time. They are asking for *the Church's established service*—hopefully highly personalized—which involves seeking the blessing of Almighty God upon the marriage decision made between the bride and the groom.

In several of the more liturgical denominations, the selection of the type of service is a moot point—for example, Catholics, Episcopalians, Lutherans, Moravians—worshipers in general know that these services have been firmly established and formalized by the Church, perhaps for several hundred years. When her Moravian grandfather died, my wife took great comfort in the knowledge that the very same funeral liturgy had been a strong support to people at the times of death for five hundred years. It was the Church's set and long-established service. If you peruse one of these services, you will find that it generally says what needs to be said on that occasion and says it pretty well. This doesn't mean that these services are unalterable in every detail. In fact, there are numbers of acceptable ways to adapt and make them more personal. But it is just not acceptable to ignore the solid principles and traditions of the Church in favor of some self-made rites. These services may be personalized, but it is destructive to alter them based simply on current fads or one's imagination, independent of their tradition and history. There is really no such thing, for instance, as an "Independent" Catholic or an "Independent" Presbyterian Church. These are further examples of connectional Churches with long and solid liturgical histories.

People know that in the Church these rites have evolved through much biblical and theological study and experience. Some basic, established principles need to be observed. One should remember that the elements of any special worship service must bear an appropriate meaning to *all* the assembled people, as well as to the primary participants. I have chosen to omit from this discussion any mention of "wedding warehouses," which include drive-in or roadside wedding chapels that attempt to give a semblance of a sacred atmosphere but which are usually aimed at what they can get rather than what they can give.

These "basic principles" to which we have just referred have largely to do with the category into which the Church puts wedding and funeral rites. I expect nobody in the crowd here to raise even an eyebrow when I fearlessly assert that both weddings and funerals are *worship services* of the Church. This is not some new idea we're talking about here. Most literature devoted to weddings or funerals makes this same assertion. We have all read that they indeed are worship services, but somehow there exists a vast difference between what we know and what we do. Such a claim is easier said then done! We're going to have to chat about that for a few minutes because a large majority of the weddings AND funeral services that I have attended over the years have very clearly *not* been worship services at all!

In reality these occasions apparently are viewed merely as sacred rituals of the Church, which attitude relegates them to an exclusive, purposeful category that is not necessarily defined as worship. We perhaps need to note here that it is certainly possible to have a wedding or a funeral that is contrary to its purpose as a worship service. In point of fact, it happens all the time, not only at the court house, but in the sanctuaries of main line Christian churches!

Not having thought about that fact, I contend, has led us into heap big trouble! Let's pull over on to a siding here and try to clarify this sad situation.

Ordinarily, when we think about a worship service of the Church, we envision the order of events that happens as we assemble in the sanctuary at the eleven o'clock hour on a Sunday morning. Now that's real worship! But, of course, the church family meets there for other occasions, too. We generally give those other gatherings different names because they have different purposes . . . fellowship suppers, Bible studies, vespers, etc. Well, weddings and funerals are surely amongst these "other occasions," and they suffer from not having been viewed as occasions for worship. It is vastly important for us to come to some common agreement on just how to describe and define a worship service.

We begin by turning to that popular storehouse of information, Mr. Webster. In the latest edition of his dictionary Webster says "a worship service is a reverent, ceremonious rendering of honor and homage to God or another deity." That's all true, but it just doesn't draw the whole picture. This definition would allow groups of people all over the world to meet regularly, do nothing, and yet gain a tax-exempt status by virtue of their claim to be a Church. This just does not tell us all we need to know on the subject.

In the handy reference book, *20th Century Encyclopedia of Religious Knowledge* (p. 1190), we find this description of just what a Christian worship service is: "Public worship consists of God's revealing His grace to a group of His children, and their responding through the faith He has inspired . . . the hour may resemble that on the mountaintop where worshipers beheld the Glory of Christ as other faces fade from view (Mt. 17). . . . On most occasions, someone guides the people to the heights . . . someone who knows the God to whom he leads and knows the hearts of those he guides—and leads them through praise, prayers, readings, and preaching, so that worship becomes a means of grace. . . ." Oh, now—that draws down our focus considerably, gives us something into which we can sink our teeth. Already I want to ask if that description resembles any weddings or funerals you have seen or performed recently. . . . God's revealing His grace and His children responding to it. Maybe I would do well to ask that same question about Sunday morning worship hour. We'll return to that vital question shortly.

Professor James F. White, in his splendid little book, *New Forms of Worship* (p. 38), has this to say on the subject: "Christian worship involves consideration of God as well as of man. When we slight either, we are not talking about Christian worship any longer . . . the theological norm is the investigation of any act of worship as to its adequacy in reflecting the Christian faith." Now, that point is really a biggie! A basic characteristic of all Christian worship is that *it reflects the Christian faith!* Is this consistently so where you go to church? Does every act of worship adequately reflect Christian faith?

While we are considering Dr. White's wise words, let's note that he further adds, "Christian worship is the deliberate act of seeking to approach reality at its deepest level by

9

becoming aware of God in and through Jesus Christ and by responding to this awareness . . . thus, Christian worship does not dispense an opiate to the people nor is it a flight from the world, but rather it is a means of being with the world and oneself at a more profound level." (p. 40). (No extra charge for including that exceptionally cogent comment.)

In an effort to refine these thoughts we look to the Scriptures and find that Matthew hits the nail right on the head when he quotes Jesus as saying, "For where two or three are gathered in my name, there I am in the midst of them" (18:20). What Jesus is NOT saying here, of course, is that He is with us *only* when he assemble in groups of two or more believers. This statement is not at all a contradiction of the biblical doctrine of the omnipresence of the Lord. He is with all of His people all the time! But then when we gather in His name, we do so expectantly, fully confident that Jesus is right there in our midst and that His presence among us is going to make a fabulous difference! If it were not so, would He have told us? There is a divine focus exhibited here.

Realizing this revelation, how in the world can a Sunday morning worship hour feature a listless, boring sermon preached to a listless, bored congregation? There always ought to be an air of excitement and expectancy when Christians assemble for true worship! Again, we can plainly see that God's children rightfully should assemble for worship purposefully and expectantly. That is just the very nature of what we do! God in Christ is there, and for a very good reason! Ponder that reality a moment! We're on the trail of discerning just what this worship is all about in the context of a wedding or a funeral. For one thing, *any Christian worship service should certainly bring to us an air of excitement!* We must realize that the Son of Almighty

10

God, the God who has always acted for a purpose, who never acts frivolously, is not there in our midst just to be hanging out! He is there to fulfill a special, divine purpose. Weddings and funerals ought always to exhibit this purpose. Always!

Now we're digging on the mother lode! This thought has to lead us to a graphic understanding of precisely what goes on in true Christian worship. Just look at what we've said:

> That . . . in any Christian worship service God is surely present in our very midst.
> . . . God in Christ is in our midst to reflect Christian faith.
> . . . God reveals His grace to us.
> . . . We ought to be able somehow to sense and be excited by His presence.
> . . . We become aware of and respond to Him.
> And that God here induces us to consider both God and man.

Part of the risk and the reward of examining so closely the dynamics of Christian worship is the possible revelation that some things that happen regularly when we assemble in God's name do not accomplish what Christian worship is purposed to do by our own definition. Perhaps we don't always reflect the Christian faith because we just have not clarified our own thinking on this subject.

Prior to leaving the examination of the nature of Christian worship, perhaps we would do well to note that the profound business of sensing His presence ordinarily has nothing to do with experiencing the revelation of never-before-known secret commands from the Almighty. Some evangelical-type preachers cause us to question the validity of our own faith because God does not constantly and clearly reveal His will to us also. For most of us most of the time, worship involves reminders of the Gospel, a renewal of the salvation events that we already know to be true. The experience is something like married love. You are a husband, and your wife already knows that you love her. She has heard you proclaim that love to her a thousand times. But that all happened yesterday, and she needs to hear it all over again—*today:* Each day in the course of human events she needs to be reminded of something she knows very well so that she can appropriately respond to it. A resounding confirmation of previously established facts! The ongoing delight of rediscovery making that which is old, new! And this news is always fresh and always good!

So, in Christian worship we have a reconsideration of the key disclosures of God's acting in history. This history began in the past and continues through the present. The worshiper comes to reaffirm and appropriately respond to the basics of his faith. Now we are ready to return to the point made (but not explored earlier in this chapter) . . . hopefully with considerably more meaning: *Weddings and funerals are both meant to be complete Christian worship services!* My plan is to establish this firm footing before sallying forth to discuss in detail the planning and make-up of these services. I don't want to appear paranoid by repeatedly asking you to sift through your mind to see if the special services you have recently witnessed fit the mold of services of worship as we have defined them. Still the question lurks as to whether or not we craft these services to fulfill adequately the basic functions of any Christian worship service. Surely you can see that there is need for vast improvement!

After comparing these elements of worship with today's weddings and funerals, I now risk being plumb insulting to someone here by asserting that *both types of services currently appear to be blatantly humanistic!* Think about it. Center stage at weddings is given by design, not to the presence of God nor the reflection of the Gospel, but to a grand procession of participants, featuring the bride all dressed in white . . . the guys all gussied up in fancy suits rented just for the occasion! Without a doubt the entire grand occasion serves to glorify the bride, who stands out in the assemblage like a burning bush! We don't wonder that none of those assembled is hardly ever moved to remark, "This service spiritually inspired me deeply," or "I sensed there the presence of the Almighty." More likely to be revealingly heard is, "That was such a sweet wedding,"or "Wasn't the bride's gown gorgeous?"

Humanism!!

Now let's take a brief glance at *a modern funeral service.* Ponder for a moment about the last few funerals you have attended. When the house lights are dimmed and the faces around the casket fade from view, *the spotlight features a dead body!* A corpse, which is the empty "house" in which the recently deceased used to live. Much attention is given to the thoroughly pagan practice of viewing this uninhabited body, which has been the object of intense labor for some cosmetologist with the hope of hearing someone remark, "This body looks real life-like." Later, someone stands up in the midst of family and friends gathered there and recites a myriad of good deeds this person performed while alive, because of which the departed certainly has earned a front row seat in Heaven! While some of what the speaker says may undoubtedly be true, the thrust of the service is clearly an unbiblical emphasis on "salvation by works," which we should judge to be baseless and beside the real point of Christian worship. No matter how long is the list of good deeds done by this recently deceased person, he/she is still a sinner "saved only by the grace of our Lord Jesus Christ appropriated through faith"! Period! Isn't that the essence of our faith? Again, one who comes to a modern-day funeral to worship would be justified to ask, "Where in all of this spectacle is the witness to the saving grace of our Lord Jesus Christ held up?" Again, *humanism!!*

The special services as printed in *The Book of Common Worship* are bare bones types of renditions meant to be fleshed out and built upon. In the following chapters we'll look at suggestions of ways to enliven them and fashion them into what we have described as true worship services.

2

The Pastor's Part in Special Services

What, we may ask, is the minister's role in the planning and leadership of weddings and funerals? And what can we do to improve the entire set-up? Before you skip this portion of the book, consider the possibility that the answer to this question is neither simple nor obvious. It will not be possible to yield an absolutely definitive answer due to the diverse sizes and customs of churches being addressed here. Some larger churches, for instance, have someone on staff with the responsibility of meeting with families, hammering out the basic schemes of special services and possibly even presiding over rehearsals of weddings. That staff member would do well to consider the things about which we now talk. But the main purpose here is to address the roles being filled by ministers and worship committee members of smaller congregations who generally see the arrangements for these services through from beginning to end.

First and foremost, without delay *you can begin long range planning by teaching theology as it applies to these special worship services.* One thing I long ago realized: When someone in the congregation dies, it is too late to teach the theology of funerals—or at least the timing is not right. The same thing is true about weddings. When someone comes to you and says, "I'm ready to be married," she's probably pretty well set on what she expects the service to look like. You're asking for an unnecessary amount of conflict and tears if you get your back up and begin to veto all of her preconceived ideas that are out of accord with the teachings and traditions of the Church.

One way to get started on long range planning is to approach your ruling board at a time when there is no wedding or funeral on the horizon and suggest that they *adopt some policies concerning the special services* of the Church. When I last moved to a new pastorate and there was no big log jam of pressing business before the ruling board, I noted that the church had no written policies about anything . . . to whom the church sends flowers at a time of death, the use of the church building . . . nothing! The ruling board agreed to start a file of such policies if I would bring a rough copy of one each month for them to discuss and hopefully to adopt. I consulted the files of several other churches. As it turned out, we provoked some excellent discussions on the theology of these special services. We publicized the actions of the monthly meetings of the ruling board by posting their minutes on the church bulletin board and by running relevant items in the church news letters. That created a good deal of additional positive discussion throughout the church. Occasionally, additional news items on these subjects appeared in subsequent newsletters.

Next, *schedule programs with the young folks* of the church on the subject of love and marriage, the wedding service included. Then, when one of them comes to you later to talk about getting married, you won't have to start from scratch. A good discussion of death and funerals would play a similar preparatory role in Short Range Planning.

So, we've very briefly looked at the task of long-range planning for the church's special services.

Now for a thought or two *about short range planning.* The policy papers for the denomination with which I am affiliated [Presbyterian Church (USA)] historically has assigned the basic responsibilities for the leadership of all of its services to the clergy.

More about this will be detailed in the next chapter, but the wedding plans most often create an awkward situation right at this point. The bride-to-be usually has enlisted a relative or a friend to be her "wedding director," a person who may have had no experience at all with planning for weddings and has not been given a "job description." Often I have found that this person assumes that the job of "wedding director" is to tell everybody in the wedding party where to stand and what to do. Generally the "wedding director" is very much relieved when told by the pastor, "I have sat with the bride and groom for several hours and planned their wedding service in minute detail. If you are the director, then I am the executive producer. It is the director's job to assist the executive producer in every way possible."

I have a print-out with the director's job description on it, which is shared with all those involved as far ahead of rehearsal time as possible. Do consider handing wedding directors such a copy of the job description of your own making. We'll have considerably more to say about this down the road a piece, including a sample print-out of instructions for the director.

PART TWO

The Wedding Service

3

The Planning of a Wedding Service

The Initial Contact

Just a little sidebar here—Sometimes it is a parent who first calls the church to inquire if the pastor will consent to perform the wedding of the daughter of the family. Before things go any further, my usual response is: "Wow! It sounds like some big news in the making over at your house! You just tell your sweet daughter to call me at her first opportunity, and we'll just set up a date to talk about it." That reply fits the bill even if the daughter is living out of town and generally meets with a positive response. Be it known that I want to deal with the engaged couple first hand. For one thing, it cuts down on later surprises. Of course, sometimes circumstances dictate that the bride-to-be has to make this initial contact alone. At any rate, that first phone call preliminary to my initial appointment does not necessarily yield a yes or no response to the question of whether or not I will consent to perform this wedding. The climax of the conversation is the invitation, "Come talk to me about it, and we'll see if the way be clear for this wedding to take place here."

There just may be legitimate reasons why a pastor will not consent to take part in a wedding.

1. Maybe *the couple's schedule* requires that they be

married on a date on which the church has already dock-eted a sizable event, or the preacher has made plans to be in Hong Kong or some other place on the other side of the world.

2. On the other hand, you may discover later that one or both of the couple have been on a matrimonial merry-go-round and give every indication of continuing trouble, and you cannot in good conscience be a part of their wedding. In fact, there are still some denominations and some individual ministers who do not believe in the validity of divorce for any reason. I am in accord with the official teaching of my denomination, which puts the re-sponsibility on the pastor to decide *whether or not to partic-ipate in the marriage service of a divorced person.* On the one side of the issue are those who believe that the spouse who discovers that the marriage was an intolerable mistake still has to continue to endure it for a lifetime, as duly promised, even if the marriage is dead and the relationship is damaging to both parties. On the other hand, the idea of forgiveness of a child of God may reign supreme and a "fu-neral" (divorce) is held for the dead marriage with every ef-fort made to salvage the lives of the two individuals involved. One must decide which of the two is the more important: the marriage, or the lives of the two people who make it up. At any rate, you can see the rub here.

3. It is possible that the prospective wedding couple who have come for counseling are—in this day and age—of the same sex. The whole idea of *same sex marriages* is a hotly debated subject right now, even among some main-line Churches. I have no intention of trying to settle that continuing issue; however, I need to point out here that the definition of marriage put forth by Webster's New Univer-sal Unabridged Dictionary describes marriage this way: "The social institution under which a man and woman es-

tablish their decision to live as husband and wife by legal commitments, religious ceremonies, etc." This description correctly defines marriage for me. There surely are people who are homosexual, and there are surely homosexuals who have a close relationship. I do them no dishonor when I affirm the opinion that theirs is not a marriage by any definition I know. I would decline to take part in a ceremony in which their relationship would be called a "marriage."

4. The pastor just may discover family turmoil that is sufficient to warrant his/her backing off from being part of this service at the time. Oftentimes there is a pronounced difference of opinion between the kind of service the young couple wants and the kind the mother of the bride wants. I must confess to playing favorites here. It seems most important to me to please the bride and groom if it can be done without magnifying the family conflict. There was a mother who wanted to stage a huge blast to celebrate her daughter's wedding. She intended to invite her business associates from all over the world and possibly outer space. The bride and groom confided to the pastor that they very much wanted to invite only relatives and a few close friends for a more intimate setting. I'm not telling you what a poor job I did dealing with the above situation. But you as a minister, now have the advantage of previewing the possibility of such a conflict early on and thus being prepared to negotiate some satisfying compromises. Be ready to face the parental question: "I'm paying for the wedding. Does it not seem fair to you that I should have the say-so about what kind of wedding it will be?"

My reaction to that question is to ask, "If there is a conflict of interests involved in the planning for a wedding, whose desires should have priority . . . the bride and groom or the parents? It's a family choice."

5. Sometimes this item becomes a bar to further dis-

cussions: A good idea is to *make it known to the bride and groom from the get-go that you insist on having an unspecified number of pre-marital counseling sessions with them,* which is tantamount to their taking your course on "Love and Marriage!" If they are unwilling or unable to comply, I simply point out that there are a number of pastors in every community who will schedule a wedding (for a fee) with a couple coming to them right off the street. Not all pastoral counselors believe in the worth of these pre-marital sessions, but I very definitely do! Also, there is not a universally accepted agenda to be followed when a young couple does come to the church office to talk about getting married . . . nor is there one for the sessions that follow. It mostly involves discussing what experience has taught you is important and utilizing your natural social skills. If you dread visiting and think constantly of other things you could best be doing, this will prove to be a difficult task for you.

Perhaps you have read recently about seminars of pastors meeting to discuss ways to reduce the ridiculously high number of divorces currently bedeviling marriages. One of the major recommendations they make to pastors: Always insist on well-planned pre-marital counseling sessions! I most heartily agree.

Considerable homework is required of you. If it is fun and interesting for you, it will be evident to the couple. What now follows is one person's suggestion of a pre-marital counseling agenda. You may prefer your own, or some variation of this one, so add to it or subtract from it as you will. The important thing here is that it gives you a starting place, something to think about. Also, some denominations have excellent materials to guide your thoughts and actions with a couple about to be married.

4

The Pastor and the Couple

The Welcome

After the couple is welcomed and seated, discover just who they are and what they have in mind. Here is where you begin to learn things about them that give you a clue as to how their courtship is going, what marriage means to them, and whether or not either of them has previously been married. If they do not have a close relationship with the Church, talk to them about why they approach the Church when it comes time to be married. They may be expecting that God will magically show His favor to a marriage generated in a church. Incidentally, I began to charge a small fee to conduct the weddings of non-church members when I discovered that couples were coming to me for their weddings when they found out that I did not charge them anything. But I have often consented to take part in the wedding of an unchurched couple just for the opportunity to relate to them things about the faith and about the Church. I never make my participation conditional upon their promise to become new church members, but I do require them to hear about the faith, whether or not they take it home to keep.

In these sessions is where you ask personal questions, none of which would be any of your business if you were not discussing marrying them . . . questions like, "Have your ever been married before? If so, what happened? Was this a divorce? Or, is the former spouse deceased? Do you have any children?" Somewhere along the way you will want either to commit yourself with pleasure to conducting their wedding rites or decline their invitation with deep regrets.

Logistics

Find out about some of the logistics of the planned wedding. Get any basic information needed. Discuss the proposed date and time of the wedding so that the church calendar and that of the pastor can be checked out and the appropriate facilities reserved. In case the couple shares with you that they are already expecting a baby, you should be sensitive to their situation and to the possibility that an early wedding would help them get married life started a little easier. This discovery would also impact your pre-marital counseling topics. Incidentally, I always have something to say to the couple about approving the proper order of events . . . marriage first! But having shared this witness, I don't dwell on it.

Determine the Desired Location of the Wedding

Many a pastor has been surprised to find out as the wedding date nears that the couple has not planned to be married in the church sanctuary, but rather in the church chapel, or the church yard, or the park out on the edge of town. You just may need to scrap your vision of how the ceremony will be done and start over from scratch!

Review with Them the Church's Basic Wedding Policies

Get all of these matters out in the clear early in the game, because the couple may be displeased and decide to go elsewhere for their nuptials. They will learn that certain practices are not okay in this church. These may include such things as involving non-sacred music, moving or putting tacks or nails in the church furniture, including an animal wedding party member (Don't laugh!), etc. Also, you need to share with them whether or not any fees will be due the church—for the use of the church facilities, the services of the sexton, the organist—and if so, when these fees will be due. Many churches require certain fees for the use of the church building and that all fees be paid in full on or before rehearsal time.

Here comes another sidebar, this one concerning fees: Not too many people agree with me on this point, but the discussion is worth the struggle! The call of a minister to be the pastor of a church includes a whole sweep of duties. Those duties, for which the pastor is paid regularly, include conducting worship, preaching, visiting, counseling, baptizing, serving communion, burying the dead, marrying—to name the most prominent of them. In crass terms, these are the kinds of things that pastor is *paid* to do. He does not get paid a bonus on any occasion because he performs any one or all of them particularly well. It would be improper, for instance, for a church member to come up after a Sunday morning service and say, "Preacher, that was an extra good sermon today. Here is $10." The preacher is already getting paid to preach, and any additional funds accepted for doing that task would be double dipping. You see where I'm headed here. I always share with the couple at this first session the fact that *I neither expect nor will I accept an honorarium* for performing the wedding of members. I was once out fishing with a fellow gentleman of the clergy when I aired my ideas on not taking any fees for weddings, and he adamantly disagreed. "Your people will never appreciate your not taking an honorarium," was his retort. My reply was that it was not a question of whether or not they would appreciate my refusal to take an honorarium, but it is a question of what is right! I already get paid for doing all the pastoral things, weddings included.

Sure, you're going to spend a pretty good chunk of time with the bride and groom. But then occasions arise when you will spend extra time with almost every member of your congregation, most often in times of trouble. But that's all a part of the job. Besides, when are you NOT on the clock? One of the possible advantages of openly dealing with this matter early on is that it erases any question about your motives for doing extra things for them. You know how you wonder about the motives of a serving person who buzzes around your table anxiously inquiring if everything is to your satisfaction? Is she really concerned for your welfare, or is she only after a bigger tip? You can take the question off the table for the bride and groom. . . .
Oh, I know I'm bucking tradition here. Traditionally, the Best Man slips the preacher a few bucks at the reception, and then the preacher passes the money-loaded envelope on to his wife for the purpose of "buying herself a new hat." Some pastors I know generally send the bride and groom a post-wedding note and enclose their honorarium with the instructions to use it for some new pleasure. The question is a thorny one and your reaction to it depends on how close you and the couple have bonded during the counseling sessions. Anyway, if the young couple intended suitably to reward you monetarily for the time and effort you

put forth during the considerable number of hours you have spent with them in preparation for their marriage, their $25 gift to you would be downright insulting.

Make appointments for further discussions. You may have a certain number of counseling sessions in mind. My usual procedure is to make a date for that first appointment and then set a regular schedule for the subsequent sessions. Sometimes questions arise that will lead to more sessions than you had originally intended. I find that it is best to start the pre-marital sessions at least six months before the wedding date, so that you can complete them far enough ahead to stay clear of the pre-wedding time crunch. It seems good ordinarily to schedule about one session per week, each of an hour's duration. If the sessions get longer than that, you cover more ground than the couple can digest. If the groom is coming from out of town, you'll surely want to accommodate the couple by scrunching up the sessions into a condensed time frame.

Pencil in plans for the wedding rehearsal. (The suggestion to use a pencil is made because the very likely possibility of having to change these plans along the way somewhere is great.) Set it at a time when the wedding party will be able to be present . . . after, not before, quitting time on Friday, for instance. By the way, it is a curious fact that not one single time in all my years of ministry have I ever been able to start rehearsals at the hour set, and I have always been on time! Someone essential to the occasion has always been late. I always assure them that this is not a real bother to me because I have marked off the entire evening for this occasion. Anyway, it is usually planned for the night before the wedding, before or after the rehearsal dinner.

There are alternatives you can suggest in case some of the party can't get into town until the day of the ceremony.

On one such occasion the wedding party was being given a noon luncheon on the wedding day. It was a simple matter to arrange for everyone to drop by the church an hour before the luncheon and get the dandy deed done then. If it is well organized, a rehearsal should not ordinarily take more than an hour.

By the way, now is a good time to check with the couple to find out for what occasions your presence will be expected and whether or not your spouse is invited. Sometimes the wedding party will be celebrating a homecoming of a sort and will appreciate having some quality time to themselves alone. Sometimes the bride and groom will assume that you know that you are expected to be present for the rehearsal dinner, for instance. It is undeniably good to get the ole calendar straight ahead of time.

5

Pre-Marital Counseling Sessions

(Part of this section will be somewhat redundant and is included here only to keep related matters together.)

DO insist that they take place! I have already stated that I require them. This is true even if either of the couple has been married before. I want to explore the dynamics of the first marriages to discover what they've learned from them that are constructive lessons for this marriage. A discussion of sex is not in any case excluded. What couples did not learn with their former spouses is often a surprising and fruitful subject. There are some splendid little pamphlets about marriage on the market which can serve as discussion starters. Put some such literature in their hands with the request that they read it separately or together before the session. I emphasize having these sessions even though I am aware that some bright counselors deny their worth. Those on the negative side of things feel that spouses-to-be are too emotionally fired up to be able to concentrate on a pastor's imposed agenda. There is surely some truth in what these folks say, but it only serves to underscore the importance of the counselor's approach. If the counselor puts a good deal of time and thought into constructing relevant and zestful sessions based on his/her own experience in working with people and the discovery of the interests and the needs of each couple, then he/she has a remarkable opportunity to energize the couple and spawn something fruitful about which they may think. It is often true that these counseling sessions don't introduce all new material to the couple but rather tend to motivate them to explore helpful ideas that may have previously escaped their notice.

Start the sessions as far ahead of the wedding date as possible. If it is to be a June wedding, I prefer to begin the sessions around January so that we will not be rushed in order to cover the territory and so that we can finish our sessions satisfactorily, even if it is necessary to miss a week or two. The bride and groom's schedule usually gets a little hectic as the wedding date gets close, so it is helpful to them if these appointments don't make their days even more crammed. I always try to make it easy for them to call and re-schedule with me if anything comes up. Again, if the bride reveals that she is expecting a child and that she is anxious for the counseling sessions and the wedding date to be moved up as much as practical, it would be well to accommodate her as far as you can.

Set your own number of sessions—one hour each. In the past I've tried to suggest to a couple that we spend five sessions together. That has usually worked out pretty well. But sometimes they ask a good question concerning a matter that you have not fully covered with them or even on a subject that was not a part of your agenda. It may become apparent to you that an unplanned hour would be beneficial. Sometimes it is better not to cover all of the material planned for one hour. By the way, if they broach questions that are beyond my knowledge and experience, I have sometimes referred couples to a retired accountant or physician for their help. Not many years ago young couples were required by some states to have a pre-marital physical examination before they could obtain a marriage license. It is still a good idea to suggest that couples-to-be do this in order to assure that they give their healthiest selves to each other in marriage.

I'm suggesting that *each session* be *no longer than an hour in length.* That has a couple of advantages. For one thing, it continues to surprise me how much meat from the sessions is "digested" by the couple later on. You can take up enough material in an hour together for them to have plenty to chew on later. Good hour-long sessions do spur interesting conversation for them later. And then, it is a courtesy to the couple to have some indication as to how much time their appointments with you will take just in case they have other activities planned after you are finished with them for the day.

Some denominations have splendid pre-marriage curricula. You can obtain these materials in a Church bookstore or catalog. They will furnish you with a study guide and some material to put into the hands of the couple. Look over these materials ahead of time. You will want to add to some chapters and perhaps subtract from others.

If you're formulating your own agenda, here are some suggested topics to include:

1. Review your understanding of the wedding location. It pays to be sure that you are all on the same page.

2. Remind them that the wedding is by and large the Church's service. Point out again that there are a number of ways to personalize it—the selection of music, scripture readings, the homily, using their names in the ceremony instead of "this man" and "this woman," etc. We will detail those items later.

3. Assure the couple that you desire to help them do things to their satisfaction, while making certain that everything about the wedding service has theological integ-

rity. You want to help them do what they want to do and help them do it right!

4. Speak to them of The Nature of Marriage. There is surely more than one way to look at marriage, but it means a lot to me to point out that **marriage is a living thing**! I take quite literally the expression which says, "Joe and Jane went to the church where they were UNITED in marriage." They entered the church that day as individuals, but they emerged from the church as Joe and Jane Jones, a brand new composite person making an appearance in the world for the very first time ever. As they then go down the street, people will say, "There go The Joneses." They will never cease to be Joe and Jane, but now they also are the Joneses "until death do us part." That means that the marriage ceases to exist only upon the death of either Joe or Jane.

That we all understand. **BUT** it is also possible for the marriage, which has been so full of life, to expire while Joe and Jane are still alive. In a very real sense, that is also a form of death. Marriage can die like a vine entwining a tree. The host lives on even when the vine dies. We live in a world where such tragic things do sometimes happen—and not all that infrequently!

Now give ear to this: The Church historically has opposed divorce. Once upon a time most ministers would not (or could not) re-marry anyone who had been divorced. Not everyone understands why; but you and I are now in the process of exploring that reason. It comes down to this: In the Ten Commandments the Bible says, *"Thou shalt not do murder."* Well, the one who is responsible for the demise of a living marriage is breaking that commandment! **That person is willfully ending a life—by murder!** Then comes a divorce, which is as devastating as a funeral. (Ask any divorced person.) As is said near the conclusion of the traditional marriage service, "Whom God has joined together let no human being put asunder." There are some church groups who believe that even if a marriage does die, the man and woman composing that marriage ought to continue to live on with the corpse. They do not believe in having a "funeral" (divorce) for a dead marriage. I take my stand along with the denomination to which I belong. I mourn the death of any marriage. When it is ended, I favor doing my utmost to help salvage and rehabilitate the two lives that make it up, helping to aid their repentance and their embarking on life anew.

Either view takes marriage quite seriously. What I have briefly described better fits my personal theology and my perception of reality.

5. *Marriage in its essence centers around mutual love and mutual trust.* Read Ephesians 5:21–32. How many times have you heard that passage interpreted from the pulpit as saying only, "Wives, subject yourselves to your husbands?" For crying out loud, look at and consider the entire passage rather than just looking only for the words which will bolster what you already believe! The passage tells husbands AND wives to give themselves to each other as Christ gave Himself to the Church. So, you would properly define married love as mutual subjection, mutual sacrifice, and mutual satisfaction. Perhaps those characteristics are most clearly seen in the act of love itself. When just the sex act occurs without these characteristics . . . well, that's something that lower animals do. The act of love is something that men and women do mainly for the satisfaction of their partners, which greatly heightens their own satisfaction. We mentioned the fact that mutual trust is the essence of married love. Listen: **A lot of mistakes can be made in the course of a marriage; but if trust still abides, then there remains something solid with which to work toward rehabilitation.** There remains hope! Without

this trust, get ready for a funeral performed in memory of that marriage.

One can see here the terrific damage that is done to a marriage when one of a couple cheats on the other. We make it sound trivial and harmless by saying that he or she "had an affair." We make it sound so very common, like something that will be quick and easy to smooth over . . . simple to confess and simple to forgive, like a twenty-four hour virus. Well, this just is not so! Once trust is destroyed or even bent out of shape, it is really tough to restore. It may be harder starting all over again.

Well, you can see where this line of reasoning comes from and where it is headed. It is a very important to explore with the couple this whole question of "What is this thing called love?" so that they can work on it daily.

6. Discuss *some common areas of marital conflict.*

Emphasize the importance of *in-house communication.* Another thing that distinguishes the human animal from the lower ones is the ability to communicate precisely what is on our minds. If I have the desire and if I really try, I can accurately project my thoughts and attitudes to you, even if I am not very articulate! Not everyone really tries! Some folks just give up too easily on their spouses. Wives and husbands often don't have a clue to what is on one another's mind. That happens for various reasons. For one thing, we become accustomed to saying to ourselves things we ought be saying to each other.

Example:

A certain husband is unusually quiet at the supper table. The wife asks, "Have I done something to make you angry?" And he thinks to himself, "How could she think she's done something to make me angry? I just stepped in the door from work, and supper was on the table."

This wife has a problem: *She can't read his mind!* She will never know that he had a troublesome run-in with the boss at work today that sort of took the wind out of his sails—*unless he comes right out and tells her.* She intuitively thinks that she is the problem and wants to help solve the situation, but she never will know how to do it unless he shares with her what the problem really is. Even if he doesn't want to talk about it at the moment, he could say something like,

> "Honey, I had a bad day at the office today. It makes me feel sort of sullen. You had nothing to do with it. I'll talk to you about it later."

And then . . . the wife, knowing that her husband's favorite dessert is pecan pie, had made him one for supper. That is a real act of love! He cleans his plate but says nothing.

She finally asks,

> "Well, did you like the pecan pie?"
> Annoyed at the question, he replies, "I ate it, didn't I?"

In the arena of love and marriage, actions are certainly important, but they will never replace our lofty ability to speak of love such as,

> "Honey, I just loved that pie!" or even, "That pie was great!"
> or, "I can just taste in that pie your love, dear one!"

Again, these wives couldn't read their husbands' minds! We ought not to put them in the position of feeling guilty because of this "fault." We can avoid doing so by sharing our thoughts instead of internalizing them.

Propose the idea that their wedding should be the real beginning of their courtship. I have wondered why so many couples get along so well together before their weddings and then go into a nosedive soon thereafter. My suspicion is that they feel that the nuptials bring welcome relief from the romantic necessities of courtship. Before marriage, they exchanged flowers when there was no dance; they initiated spontaneous telephone calls to each other when there was no news to relate; they did for each other little thoughtful acts which provided constant reminders that they were each someone special. But now, after the wedding, the contest is over! They have won the prize! There now is no need to continue to compete. You have no problem seeing what the situation is. The honeymoon ends, and they begin to take each other for granted. Intimacy in their total relationship seems to cease growing. Sexual intercourse becomes the totality of intimacy. When I give to the bride and groom a copy of The Marriage Service, from which I read at their wedding, I usually write in it the words "And now the courtship really begins!"

Hopefully that leads them to reflect on some things we talked about during our pre-marital sessions together. The bottom line is that they should continue to be loving and lovely to each other throughout the years.

To Be, or Not to Be . . . *Children?*

Decisions about having children are not that simple to make. Couples keep asking questions about whether or not this cruel world is a place in which they want to bring up a child. Today, young people have active social lives, but a good many of them have put other things on the front burner besides having children. They scramble to make a place for themselves in the job market; they set goals for themselves about what position they want to achieve by their 50th birthday, or what salary level they want to reach before getting married or having children. There is so much unrealistic thought and conversation that takes place by people who have never had a child. Then, a couple's parents have their own peculiar pressure points on this subject, and they are often far from negligible. And some young people just refuse to admit that they really don't like children, or that for whatever reason they don't want to have children. Perhaps they've seen other couples have babies and then give those babies away to someone else to raise, to teach their children to walk, to hear them learn to talk, to play a formative part in their personality and character development. There is so much that is unpredictable about the future. Nobody knows how or what to choose. I was unmarried going into my thirties. Somebody advised me to get married and start a family right away lest I become a grandfather to my own children. That plan was workable for me. We discovered that there is no greater high than to be pregnant when you want to be and no deeper low than to be pregnant when you don't want to be. You can rummage around in this area of thought with a couple, but in the end, they are going to have to batten down the hatches and come up with a decision of their own.

How to Deal with *Conflict*

Most of us intuitively know how to raise a ruckus and start some kind of fight around the house—but most of us don't know much about how to end one. There are a few clues that can help. You know the routine. The squabble is usually over nothing;

It's breakfast time and he's got up on the wrong side of the bed.
"Just look at that toast. You always burn the toast!".
And she says, "Well, if you'd get to the table the first time I call you, it wouldn't ever be burned."

In the first statement he sent the ball way over the fence separating fact from fiction. His wife undoubtedly does not burn the toast EVERY time she fixes it. What he said was untrue, and it was childish. He didn't tell her what really was making him grumpy. Then the little girl in her responded to the little boy in her husband by declaring that he was always late for breakfast. Probably not true either! Someone has written that within every bride and every groom is the little girl she used to be and the little boy he used to be. What happened in this little scene is that the little boy in him surfaced and made his childish statement, and then the little girl in his wife emerged and also responded childishly. The result was that they had a childish spat, perhaps hurt each other, and the real issue never got aired and never got dealt with.

Time and again, this same scenario happens in houses in every neighborhood. The point of this exercise is to suggest to the young couple that when the child in your spouse appears, the thing for you to do is maintain your maturity until the storm blows over.

In this instance here the wife might have said something like,

"Gee, dear, I detect that you're not having a perfect morning, and I'm sorry to be part of it. We can talk about this later if you care to." Period!

Note that the wife doesn't make any accusations or charges; she doesn't provide any ammunition to make the conflict worse either; she steps away from the combat zone without losing either her temper or her dignity.

What about Church Finances, Drugs and Sex?

I'm lumping several things into this next category. Because of what you have learned about the couple you are dealing with, you may choose to expand certain items here or include others.

The Church presents a rather prominent bone of contention for newlyweds even while symbolizing peace and harmony. It is certainly appropriate to recommend to the couple that they enter into the life of some church—for social reasons, at least. Where else can they expect to meet other worthy young adults whom they can enjoy and appreciate? It is a fine idea to recommend to them that they be a part of something larger and older than themselves . . . something with a solid past and a promising future. Some young couples fail to see the worth of Church membership until they become parents and realize that they have undertaken a role that they can't handle by themselves. But the real rub comes when they discuss to which Church they are going to belong.

The world is filled with mixed marriage. . . . Catholics and Protestants, conservatives and liberals . . . and those involved often stand for principles at the opposite ends of the spectrum. To belong, or not to belong?

We bring to the altar plenty of differences that tend

eventually to pry us apart. Religion can do that also unless we prepare for the future. Now is the time to talk about such matters. The Church needs to be important to this couple . . . and they, to the Church!

Finances (and their disposition) is obviously a subject about which any couple needs to discuss and to come to some agreement. Many households rumble like thunder with disagreements over money: how is it to be saved and how it is to be spent. Several times I have referred young couples to a retired banker friend for financial advice beyond my experience. I recommend to you that maneuver if the situation calls for it. My own experience may not be helpful here—but when we were first married, my wife didn't work outside the home for pay. I fast-talked her into keeping our books, a task which she still performs. Through the years I handed my monthly paycheck to her, and she did the banking and the paying of bills.

This arrangement is not for everyone. It is one way to handle things, not THE way. Couples who are both working may, for their own reasons, choose to have separate bank accounts and, thus, separate books. Cool. For me and my house the item of mutual trust (already discussed) is a big thing. Since my wife knows our financial status better than I do, I trust her to know what we need to buy and what we can afford. I trust that she has the same financial goals as I do. I say that because I know of a couple whose purse strings are firmly controlled by the husband. He examines the books constantly and calls on his wife to justify every expense that he didn't authorize. As you can imagine, money is constantly a source of hard feelings in that household. He doesn't seem to trust her . . . is suspicious that her goal is to spend a lot while his is to save a lot. So get on the same page however you arrange things so that you can live happily—and trustfully!—ever after!

Drugs—the illegal kind—are ever more pervasive in today's world. Whether or not I am in favor of doing drugs is not the centerpiece of my discussions with young couples. Like finances, the important thing is that they both agree on whether or not the use of illegal drugs is acceptable and that whatever they do is done openly and above board. Trying to do drugs on the sly is a threat to the trust factor and has put an extra strain on many a marriage.

Sex is another area of potential conflict that needs to be addressed. Most folks who approach the marriage altar would certainly seem to know the facts of life. You would assume that is true, especially since a high percentage of them have been sexually active or even have been married before; some are pregnant already; some couples have even lived together before marriage, and some women have been on "the pill" for quite a spell. But there is so much more to understand about sex besides being able to draw a schematic of the human body. For one thing, the act of love is an action based on being *united* in marriage. He actually enters into her, and they are one! Part of the wonder of their intermingling is the realization on the part of each of them that they bring to their partner the highest caliber of pleasure and satisfaction! It is sex within marriage. It is legal. It is wonder-filled!

After years of hearing no-no, now it is yes-yes! Newlyweds need to know that there is no "normal" number of times per week that a couple has intercourse. It's up to each couple to discover what is mutually pleasing. A young couple needs to hear that kind of affirmation from a representative of the Church.

One other thing: Room ought to be reserved in a couple's love life for the kind of frankness that makes it unnecessary for either partner to fake a "headache" on a night when making sexual love is not desirable for any reason at all. Newlyweds may scurry to the bedroom at the end of every day or before, excited at the prospects of making love. They don't foresee the advent of a night when they will want to say good night with only a warm kiss, then zip off to dreamland. This is just to reaffirm that such a night will come to pass, and a bride and groom need to work out together a way for either of them to say "No!" without hurting anybody's feelings. Something like,

> "I just love you like the dickens, but tonight I'm just flat out pooped. Please don't read anything else into this script. A good ole kiss and a snuggle or two, and I am off to an exciting dream about you!"

My words don't work very well in your mouth, but you get the idea. Perhaps a good approach is to plan to make love every night before the arrival of the sandman, but such a strategy doesn't always need to involve sexual intercourse!

The above list is certainly not exhaustive, as is true about the remarks about each one. What we have here are thought starters.

The Recording of the Wedding Service (photos/films/tapes, etc.)

During the planning of the wedding service the bride and groom will certainly ask questions about whether or not the use of cameras, videos and tapes is permitted in the church during a service. The bottom line here is that nothing should be done during any worship service that distracts from the focal point of the service. Left to their own devices, photographers have been known to sabotage the wedding proceedings by running up and down the aisle and causing flash bulbs to erupt in the middle of everything. What they do can absolutely arrest the attention of everyone unless they are informed that such conduct will not be tolerated. I nearly had a conniption once when a member of the wedding congregation abruptly rose from her pew, came down front in the church, stood right next to me and took a flash snapshot of the bride and her father coming down the aisle. I was on the verge of tossing her out with the garbage when she reclaimed her seat. She was very offended when I confronted her about it later. I told her that if she would not do that at Sunday morning worship, she should not do it during this worship service either. She'll probably never go to church where I do!

During a planning session I inform the couple that flash pictures of any kind are not permitted during a wedding service. Photographs, film, and certainly audio tapes are permissible as long as a flash is not used. I relate to them that following the conclusion of the service, we will re-enact any or all of the service so that photographers may record everything desirable. I send word to the duty photographer that I desire a brief word prior to the wedding just to make sure we're all on the same page. These stipulations I re-state at rehearsals for the benefit of members of the wedding party and the duty photographer.

I bring up the subject of the Wedding Director at this stage of the planning because the bride soon needs to be lining up the wedding party, and the Director is a prominent figure in that group. The role of the Wedding Director has already been mentioned in passing, but that role needs to be detailed so that the bride understands it and can pass along her understanding to the person who consents to do this job. Her word will reinforce the minister's instructions to be offered later. Because this is an area of almost certain conflict, I usually provide a print-out detailing the Director's job description to show to the bride and to be passed on to the Director. It answers a lot of questions before concepts of the job have to be re-tooled. I shall include here a copy of that print-out just for your information. Because your procedures will differ in some aspects from mine, you will want to amend what is here. Hopefully this will be helpful.

6

The Role of the Wedding Director

Introduction

This brief description of the role of the Wedding Director is composed out of deep appreciation for the person who consents to do this important job as a favor to a good friend or relative who is planning to be married. Some larger churches have on their staffs social or wedding directors who are specialists at working with weddings and other major events. We here are obviously addressing churches that do not have such extensive staffs.

Since there is very little written about this job, everyone harbors his or her own ideas about what it involves . . . usually focusing on whatever the word "director" suggests, which is usually different things to different people. We now want to narrow it down and interpret what it should mean specifically here in the church.

Part of the confusion stems from the fact that many churches and clergymen have left the definition of the job of Wedding Director to the young couple and their helpers, who may never have done it before. Sometimes clergymen have simply surrendered their leadership responsibility because it appears as if the way in which this sacred rite is performed is someone else's task. We sometimes say, "However they want to do it, let 'em do it. It seems like it is more trouble than it is worth. Anyway, what difference does it make?" That approach often results in a Director and a pastor operating with very different goals in mind and ending up angrily getting in each other's way.

Well, it really *does* matter how you go about organizing a wedding. It is not a game of "dealer's choice", and conscientious Directors deserve to know from the start just what are the parameters of their job. They need to be informed about your denominational traditions and, again, the fact that *wedding services historically have been derived by and for the Church.* The elements of it have been chosen by the Church purposely to mold a worship service that is particularly appropriate for a wedding.

Because the service of the celebration of a wedding is of the design (not of those getting married, but of the Church), some denominations have been very specific in stating in their corporate documents that "the pastor shall have entire responsibility for the direction of the total service" [PC (USA)]. Knowing what area the umbrella of the pastor's responsibility covers should certainly take the pressure off of the neophyte Director, who usually has the impression that she (?) is accepting the awesome job of designing the entire wedding, including what everybody does, when and where they move, what they say at rehearsal, during the service, and what all goes on at the reception! The chosen Director has indeed accepted a vital, versatile job, but it has a completely different description from this one. *She is to provide whatever assistance the pastor needs before, during and after the wedding service.* And the following description will attest to the fact that those needs, although quite simple, are many and absolutely vital!

The Duties of a Wedding Director

Prior to the Rehearsal

1. *Acquaint yourself with the wedding guidelines and regulations* of the denomination (Book of Order) and the local church where the wedding is to take place to make sure you do things accordingly. There should be brief documents in the office of the church to help one do this.

2. *Consult with the pastor* to be informed about his/her expectation of your task. Feel free to ask questions and offer suggestions. A trip to the wedding site would be most helpful.

3. *Visit with the bride* about the logistics of the wedding service, such as where she wants the groomsmen and bridesmaids to stand when they process to the front of the church—males on one side; females on the other, or mixed, when to give the ushers instructions to assure uniformity of styles . . . how the congregation is to exit . . . the procedure for post-service photo session . . . plans for reception . . . etc.

During the Rehearsal

1. The pastor may begin the rehearsal by asking everyone (guests too!) to sit in the front pews of the sanctuary and introducing the Director and him/herself. Everyone else follows suit. The pastor then explains that they're all present because they care for the bride and groom and because they are to put together a service of worship. Describe the nature of the wedding service as is done earlier in these writings. Conclude with a prayer, blessing the bride and groom, their marriage, and this service of wor-

ship. This type of focus tends to exclude extreme frivolity during rehearsals.

2. Then, the pastor calls forward and places the bride and her father, the groom and best man, and the maid/matron of honor. As we said, the bride is on her father's *left* arm.

3. Next, when the pastor calls for the groomsmen and the bridesmaids to come forward, the Director should *help them line up* in the agreed-upon order and so that they will match up well when they recess at the end of the service.

4. After they talk through the service and then recess to the rear of the church, *line up the wedding party* in the foyer in the order that they will enter the sanctuary so that they will be ready to practice the processional.

5. Then stand at the sanctuary entrance ready to *start each wedding party member down the aisle* with proper spacing.

    a. **When to start them:** You need to ask the pastor about this in advance because there are different approaches. Personally, I prefer for the pastor to enter the sanctuary first, then, open the pulpit Bible (as I do). *Note:* No one starts down the aisle until the minister, the groom, and the best man have arrived at their respective positions.

    b. **Now, start the wedding party** (everyone except the bride and her father) down the aisle with agreed-upon spacing, the last of which will be the ring bearer and then the flower girl (if they are included. Help them to know where to stand down front.)

c. After the rest of the wedding party has gone down the aisle and are in place, the organ should swell and the congregation stands, led by the bride's mother or by the minister; *then the bride and her father* will be started down the aisle. The congregation continues to stand through the invocation.

6. *When they all recess at the end of the service, catch the ushers designated* to escort the mothers of the bride and groom out. Have them return down the aisle, for the bride's mother first, then the groom's mother, followed by grandmothers and any other VIPS.

7. *If the decision is made for the congregation to exit row by row,* send the two groomsmen given the task of exit marshals back down the aisle to the very first pew, where they should turn around, start back up the aisle together and signal each row to leave, one row at a time.

8. Be sure to tell everyone in the wedding party when and where to arrive at the church on the wedding day—usually an hour prior to the commencement of the service.

After the Rehearsal: Meet with Groomsmen

1. Remind them to be dressed and in the church foyer one hour prior to the service.

2. Affirm those who will usher the wedding party, moms and any other VIPs in and out.

3. Decide who will perform the acolyte duties.

a. Pick one or two groomsmen to be acolytes.
b. Usually the candles are lit about 20 minutes before service (or, before the crowd arrives).

4. Give a crash course on ushering and escorting. (This is often overlooked!)

    a. Let one of the ushers practice by escorting the Director part way down the aisle, twice—once to a pew on each side of the aisle.

    b. Each female guest is to be escorted, always on usher's right arm, inviting her male companion(s) to follow.

    c. Each male guest not accompanying a female is to be ushered, not escorted, of course.

    d. Each guest is to be asked "How far down the aisle?" Not "Which side?" The families and friends are all to be united by the marriage!

    e. Early arrivals should not be asked to move over for folks arriving later!

Prior to the Wedding Service: The Day of the Wedding

1. The Director should *arrive at the church a little over an hour prior* to the beginning of the service.

2. *Check* to determine whether or not *all the flowers* have been delivered. See that those for the bride and her attendants get where they belong. Also, see that the other flowers get where they belong—including boutonnieres for the groomsmen and corsages for the mothers. If needed, help pin them on.

3. Decide when and how the candles are to be lit. *Remind the acolytes.*

    a. Usually this is done 15/20 minutes before service or before many guests arrive.

b. Usually light the altar candles first and then move outward from the center.

c. Done in unison if done by two groomsmen.

4. Ten minutes prior to service, see that appointed persons *go after the mothers* and other VIP's and escort them to the church foyer. Groom's mother escorted into sanctuary first; bride's last.

5. *Summon the wedding party to the foyer,* and line them up in order of their entrance into the sanctuary.

During the Wedding Service Itself

The job of the Director at this point has been fairly well defined at the rehearsal.

1. Stand at the sanctuary door, *start and space wedding party* down the aisle only when the minister, the groom, and the best man are all standing in their positions.

2. When the aisle is clear, the organ swells, and the congregation stands; *straighten the bride's dress and start the bride* and her father down the aisle.

3. *If there are late-comers,* seat them quickly and quietly near the back of the sanctuary.

4. *When the wedding party recesses . . .*

a. Remind them where to go—usually back to the sanctuary for photo session.

b. Catch the ushers of the mothers, grandmothers, any other VIP—bride's mother first!

c. Send "exit ushers" down the aisle if the congregation is to leave one pew at a time.

d. If the reception is to be at another site, the bride and groom MAY want to receive the guests as they depart from the sanctuary.

5. After the photo session, see that all candles and lights are extinguished.

6. As has been said, the job of the one chosen to be the Wedding Director is a really big one. The duties will vary from place to place, but hopefully the basics are described here. Good luck.

Somewhere along the way, the pastor needs to update the bride's mother on plans being made, which point has been made previously. If you have been working with the bride and groom on the wedding plans, do not fail to make an intentional effort to inform the bride's mother about the decisions made. This is worth repeating. It is a mistake to assume that good communication is going on at their home. Failure to heed this warning may result in dire circumstances.

A certain minister had met with a couple four or five times in the process of making plans for their wedding. Along the way they had discussed the wedding of the bride's older sister, but this couple wanted their own style of service. Everyone was stunned when the bride's mother stood up at the rehearsal with no warning and loudly proclaimed, "What you all have planned apparently is not the same as the wedding service of my older daughter. I have always tried to treat them exactly the same. For that reason this service is going to be identical to the one her sister had." The bride said nothing. The minister gave brief thought to refusing to take part in the service as amended, but he relented and performed the service that the mother wanted rather than taking a chance on causing an even worse scene. The minister then and there resolved to inform the bride's mothers in future weddings about plans being made. A word to the wise . . .

7

The Marriage License

This is the final item under "The Planning of the Wedding Service" found in the "odds and ends" file under the heading of "The Marriage License." I have found it a helpful practice to hand an information sheet about the marriage license to the couple during their first session in my office. A little research will supply the specifics. They'll know how much time they have to do what all needs to be done. The facts and figures may be different where you live, but this sample will give you an idea of what you may want to include:

Information about the Wedding License

1. The marriage license must be purchased at the Register of Deeds' office **in the same county** where the wedding is to take place.
2. Things to take with you when you go to purchase the license:

   a. ***Identification papers***
   b. If you are 21 years old or over—***Your driver's license***
   c. If under 21—***Your birth certificate***

d. The **_$40 fee_** (Of course the cost could vary)

3. The license must be purchased **within 60 days** of the wedding date (N.C.).

In most states, following the purchase of the license, there is no waiting period required, which means that the marriage can take place any time during the 60 days following the purchase of the license.

4. The marriage license is to be delivered to the officiating minister at the wedding rehearsal, or before.

5. The minister, then, is responsible for checking the data on the license, filling it out, getting it signed by witnesses, and returning it to the Register of Deeds after the wedding.

6. Most states require on the license the signatures of two local witnesses present at the wedding service.

8

The Purpose of the Wedding Service

We need to remind ourselves of *the nature and purpose of the wedding service* because it is not commonly understood. It's not that difficult to grasp, but it seems that not everybody on the block lies awake nights thinking about it. We're concerned here with a Christian worship service, which is an event where God in Christ is in our very midst to reflect Christian faith. Surely this is not a difficult environment for us to create.

Just what all is supposed to happen in a wedding service when you boil it down to its very essence? As far as the laws of the State are concerned, all that is necessary for us to do is to fulfill the barest requirements of a simple contract. This would involve the two principal parties, the bride and the groom, expressing their intentions to be married to one another on the specified day—a meeting of the minds—in the presence of an official of the state, in this case, a duly ordained minister. The signatures of two local witnesses may be required on the license.

That describes all that is necessary in the making of a legal marriage contract. We bring the marriage ritual into the Church because we want something sacred to happen, something above and beyond just legalizing the arrangement. Prior to coming to the church, something of the essence has taken place with the couple. They have mutually made a life-long, life-affecting decision in which each has given birth to the considered thought, "Before me stands the one to whom I want to be married, the person whom I want to enjoy to the fullest the rest of my life!"

Though rarely so tagged, that decision has a name. It is called *Marriage!* Now the committed couple comes to the church, traditionally before that decision is physically consummated, for a marriage service seeking God's blessing of that marriage decision in the environment of a Christian worship service.

From that less-than-adequate explanation, the description in Chapter I of the adaptation of the traditional marriage service found in the *Book of Order* begins to make sense. The wedding service should look, sound, and be a service that is both Christian and worship. This does not mean that all Christian worship services have to be the traditional type, or even be identical. What it does mean is that they need to identify and adhere to the basic principles of Christian worship we've already discussed. Incidentally, in talking with couples I usually do not discuss in detail the fact that the wedding service will be adapted for worship. I do sound them out about their preference of either the traditional or a more modern form of service. Here is what I mean when I say that the wedding service will be adapted more appropriately for worship.

This is an outline of the traditional wedding service found in the *Book of Order:*

The Opening
The Charge
The Betrothal Vows
The Parents' Approval
The Wedding Vows
The Exchange & Blessing of the Rings

The Wedding Decree
The Wedding Prayer
The Benediction

Now, in accord with what we have said concerning having a Christian worship service appropriate for a wedding, the following are the bare bones, traditional service taken from the halls of the court house and into the sanctuary of the church house:

A Service of Worship
Uniting in Christian Marriage
Joe Smith and Jane Jones

*   *   *

The Program of Wedding Music
The Processional
The Opening
The Call to Worship
The Invocation
The Statement of Purpose

The Betrothal Service
The Betrothal Vows
The Betrothal Prayer

The Word Heard
The Reading of the Written Word
The Homily

(Special Music)

The Marriage Service
The Wedding Vows
The Exchange & Blessing of Rings
(Special Music)
The Marriage Prayer
The Declaration of Marriage
The Charge

The Closing
The Benediction (The couple MAY kneel.)
The Recessional

The Organ Postlude

(Service may include other special music)

9

Music at a Wedding

About Wedding Music

While we're on the subject of constructing the wedding service, let me remark once again that the majority of weddings that I have recently attended are (sadly) not really Christian worship services. They have most assuredly been marriage rites, and they have been made contractually legal by the vows taken. But they have just as certainly not met the standards of a worship service. The seeds of this situation are sown long before the marriage service takes place.

Admittedly a volatile and incendiary subject, you don't need a lengthy recitation of battles fought here over wedding music. You'll get the general idea when I tell you about one bright-eyed bride-to-be quite a number of years ago who was adamant about featuring in her wedding the romantic old song, "Don't Sit Under the Apple Tree with Anyone Else but Me!" Anybody remember that musical jewel? Another bride-to-be came to see me almost a year before her wedding date because she knew that we were going to have a pitched battle over her desire to have a John Denver song ("Annie's Song") performed at her wedding ceremony.

Now, I sincerely enjoy both of those songs, but I have

at least two problems with including them in a church service: First, wedding music should be as meaningful to the entire congregation as it is to the couple being married, and then, the message of the music should be relevant to the divine purpose of the service.

Perhaps the point on which we dwell is quite clear now. We distinguished members of the clergy too often aim at the wrong target. We are convinced early on somewhere that our supreme goal is to assure that the bride *et al* are pleased with the goings on surrounding the wedding, and that the music for the occasion has only to be entertaining and perhaps loaded with personal memories. Indeed, this much is certainly true: We certainly want everyone to be pleased, and the music does need to mean something. But it needs to mean something in harmony with the purpose of the wedding service, which is to serve as **an expression of Divine Love,** not that of one human being for another.

I am NOT saying that the love of the bride and groom for each other is unimportant. It most assuredly needs to be near the core of what we do here. I am saying that when the bride and groom go to the Church to have their marriage decision blessed by God, the One whose blessing is being sought needs to be the central focus.

Again, whatever is included in the wedding ritual needs to fit the definition of worship and needs to be in accord with the purpose of that ordinance of the Church!

Chapter 15 of The Directory of Worship for the Presbyterian Church is devoted to the subject of Christian marriage. In Paragraph 215-8 it says: "Such music as accompanies the (marriage) service should be *to the glory of God who sanctifies marriage,* to which end the use of hymns by the congregation is appropriate." In the same section of this document is found the graphic statement,

"Such music as accompanies the ceremony should direct attention to God who sanctifies marriage, and special care should be taken to assure that it is suitable and relevant."

As Dr. Donald M. Wardlaw, professor of Homiletics and Worship at McCormick Seminary, writes,

"Music appropriate for any Christian rites of passage should somehow celebrate the central facts of the Good News, should hold up in praise the Christ event and its implications for the new estate into which our people pass. That is, the kerygma should come through, either explicitly or implicitly. Whether the words be Christian code words or poetry whose imagery and metaphors point to the Christian ultimates, the Gospel is to be celebrated, not just warm feelings and togetherness alone."

This is all true whether or not you are Presbyterian. Dr. Wardlaw says it well! As I said, I do enjoy songs written and sung by John Denver. The one proposed above has to do with Annie's love for Mr. Denver, which was indeed lovely, but it has zilch to do with God's love for him or for anybody else.

Then, one would take it that the other lady mentioned above and her intended had discovered during their courtship some unforgettably romantic things about love under an apple tree somewhere. Apple trees are lovely elements of God's creation whose fruit is delicious, but what do they say about God's love for us or ours for each other? Besides, neither the bride nor the groom were even going to be in the sanctuary when the song was to be rendered during the pre-service program of music, and there was no way that those who were to hear it were going to grasp its intended message.

And then, I know a lady who must have sung "I Love

You Truly" at a hundred weddings. She had a more than lovely contralto voice, and the song has a lovely sentiment. But we're in a special Church service here, and sacred music relevant to the revelation of God's love for us through Christ is peculiarly fitting for this occasion.

I know my thinking about music is rather conservative, perhaps too old-fashioned for some people. But I'm out here trying to blow the trumpet and call attention to the fact that we have drifted away from some sound principles of worship, and that these principles are not just matters of personal preference, they are of the essence and they make a huge difference! I have discovered that when you construct the special services of the Church with extra attention to the purposes of those services, they take on a new excitement, and the people who are a part of them are deeply gratified and probably don't even know why!

Lest you think that what I'm advocating here sadly narrows your choices of wedding music, note that the church or local library contain shelves of books of excellent sacred wedding music from which couples can pick for their services. There are just a myriad of good, solid choices of wedding music that will add substance to the mood and meaning of the wedding service. Music that is only sweet in sentiment or that suggests mainly some romantic feelings is, to get finally to the point, out of place in a Christian wedding service! You and your church musician ought to stand solidly together on this matter!

If one doesn't want to have a Christian wedding service, then you can legitimately celebrate the rite in the shade of some huge apple tree somewhere and include in it most anything you want.

Just another side bar: There are so many ways to utilize things in our wedding service that recall meaningful parts of our personal history and that are not really relevant to what in God's name is taking place in a wedding service, whether or not the stage is a church sanctuary. Some of those love songs could inject a certain vigorous spirit into the reception. That would be a good site also to make the grand introduction of the newlyweds, accompanied by a momentous ovation from the jubilant crowd, **"I now present to you the new Mr. and Mrs. Joe Smith!"** That is cutesy, but the prevalence of its use right there in the sanctuary after the wedding service has already been officially concluded with The Blessing (The Benediction) is flat deplorable! People don't seem to realize the lofty status or the meaning of The Benediction. **When The Benediction is rendered, the last word of this occasion has been spoken.** There is nothing left to be said or done! It is finished! Do give that some thought.

Again, do give some sober consideration to asking your ruling board to adopt some guidelines for weddings held there in the church. Such a sheet of information should be put into the hands of the bride and groom early in your talks with them so that they will know that they are not engaged in conversation with a narrow-minded pastor alone. Here is a set of guidelines you may want to use as a starter:

Music at a Christian Wedding Service

Guidelines from *The Directory of Worship*

1. The Christian marriage ceremony is a service of worship of the God who calls a man and a woman together in marriage. It shall be conducted with

reverence and shall be under the sole direction of the minister.

2. Hymns and other music should center on God and His love, not upon the wedding party or the worshiper. The focus is on God, not the bride and the groom.
3. The wedding music should direct attention to God, who sanctifies marriage, and not simply to love on a human level.
4. Special care should be taken to assure that the wedding music be suitable both to the wedding occasion and to the reverence of worship.
5. The music should focus on the themes which are inherent in a Christian marriage service—such as:
   a. God's love for us
   b. The Christian love which is the foundation of married love
   c. God's blessing on marriage
   d. The praise of God

6. Romanticized and secular ideas about love and marriage detract from the thrust of the service and should be avoided.

   So, we have come to the bottom line of this particular discussion about weddings. Before we move into a carefree examination of the make-up of the wedding service, let's pause for a moment to assess just where we are and what we have covered.

7. Hopefully we have established the fact that *the wedding service essentially belongs to the Church.* A young couple has all grades of choices to make

to personalize the marriage service, but it basically is the Church's service.

8. What happens during the service is that *the couple present themselves before Almighty God, who blesses them and the decision that they have made,* and grants them the strength to keep the vows they take.

9. The traditional experience of the Church is a theological one: A profound decision and His Blessing.

10. It is ordinarily good and proper to invite to the service all fellow church members, family, and friends. They used to call that "an open church wedding." This place is where the entire church family usually gathers to worship. You may want to choose from those listed which ones to invite to the reception.

With these things having been said, we roll up our sleeves and prepare to tackle a whole new category about the make-up of the wedding service!

10

The Make-up of the Wedding Service

The traditional wedding ceremony is composed of two distinct services, each with its own set of vows. You are most assuredly aware of this fact. You already know where the bride and groom stand during each of these parts of these rites. What you may not have fathomed is what it all historically means.

The Betrothal Service

The History of Betrothal

A majority of wedding services held today, even in the mainline churches, reveal a remarkable absence of insight as to the subtle historicity involved therein. There is a simple reason for this. In a seminary library one can find numbers of articles on the history of the wedding, but virtually nothing on the history of the wedding service itself. Delving into the meaning and background of this special worship service will impact greatly the way we regard and order the wedding party during the ceremony. It will likely change the way we think about what we do.

In order to understand the present-day wedding service, we need to explore a little bit of the history of the meaning of the state of betrothal.

Customarily I share the following explanation with the bride and groom during our pre-marital conversations and then briefly review these facts with the wedding party at the rehearsal just for their information. That procedure most assuredly broadens their awareness of what happens during the wedding service and just may have a positive effect on some future weddings of those in the wedding party.

Throughout history a girl has always been owned by someone else. This we have often been told. Early in her life, that someone was usually her father, the head of the household. When she became of age—usually around twelve or thirteen years—the father began the diligent hunt for a suitable mate for her. I mean, the young gal of the house didn't plow in the fields, nor did she tend the flocks; and all in the house took note of the fact that she consumed an awful lot of vittles! Just as a practical matter, something needed to be done about her living and eating arrangements.

At a glance, one can see that a marriage generally took the form of a business deal. In truth, in those days romantic love had yet to be invented. It was a foreign concept. Most marriages were arranged by two fathers whose offspring had yet to meet. So, in days of old when knights were bold, when the young people were still strangers to each other *the fathers began to work out an arrangement,* which in fact was the preliminary stage of marriage: This less-than-completely-understood state was called *"betrothal."* The word "betrothed" and the word "espoused" are synonyms. The story of the nativity of Jesus has made us somewhat familiar with these terms, for Luke tells us (Luke 2:4–5) that Joseph went up into Bethlehem to be taxed with Mary his *espoused* wife, or as the RSV puts it, "with his betrothed." Currently, a term of our courtship vocabulary, "engaged," captures a part of what we mean here, but only a part. An engaged couple exercises a claim upon each other. They grant each other exclusive rights. They declare to the world their intention to get married, usually within a specified time frame.

As has been said, in earlier times espousal was in fact the earliest stage of marriage itself, even though the young couple generally did not yet live together. An espoused couple was not just promised to one another at some future time; they were immediately bound to each other. They were yet sexually to consummate their new relationship, but betrothal was a binding agreement, the breaking of which required a divorce.

This is the big point toward which we have been fearlessly moving. *The betrothal rite historically was held at a different time (six months to two years before) and at a different place from the wedding itself.* Both arrangements were legally binding.

While we're at it, we should note that in those earlier times the groom usually initiated the rite of betrothal by pouring a cup of wine, drinking one-half of it, and setting the other half-cup before his intended. If she then drank the rest of the wine, the couple was straightway betrothed. Plans could then begin for the marriage feast, which was the form taken by the marriage ceremony itself.

The period of time between the betrothal and the wedding feast afforded the fathers the opportunity to work out the matters of the dowry. During various periods of history this transaction featured the father of the bride paying so many head of cattle, or other gifts, to the groom's father; at other times, it was the other way around. A "bride price" was required to make the betrothal legal. Incidentally, from this practice we have inherited "the gift of engagement," which usually is in the form of a ring. If things subsequently go sour, the simple return of the ring should signal the termination of the engagement. No lasting problems. No harm done.

In that patriarchal society the father was the one person who decided when everything had been properly done and all was in readiness for the wedding feast to take place. The son could then bring his bride home, which was the eventual goal here. Hear the words of the New Testament narrative suggesting the process about which we speak: "In my Father's house are many rooms; if it were not so, would I have told you that I go to prepare a place for you? . . . I will come again and will take you to myself, that where I am you may be also." (John 14:2–3) Preparations for the great heavenly wedding feast! The time for which only the Father knows. The entire marriage process presents a pattern leading to the Father.

This series of events is not an earth-shaking revelation! These days we are breaking no ancient laws by following today's customary events. But understanding the origin of these rituals deepens our perception of just what is actually happening in the traditional wedding service and helps us to grasp correctly the symbolism of the occasion. It will enable us rightly to interpret the pageantry of this sacred rite of the Church and to avoid simply reading it unabridged from the printed page, perhaps bending it to the fancy of someone in the wedding party.

It would be helpful now for you to *open a copy of the traditional wedding service* found in the Book of Common Worship or elsewhere. Note that, after the service gets under way and the wedding party is standing down front be-

71

fore the minister, the ceremony proceeds with the first of two rituals, two sets of vows, to which the groom and the bride each answer in turn, "I do" or "I will." *These are the betrothal vows,* posing the dramatic climax of the betrothal service, all of which, again, took place at a different time and place in days of yesteryear.

But now hear this: This day in time, these two important rites have been preserved and combined, both now taking place on the very same day within the same sacred hour. *At this point in the service,* the bride and groom are officially betrothed!

Well, now, we've spent an awful lot of time and energy delving into all of this wedding history. We've dug up and fertilized its roots. It is due time to stop and ask the question, "So what!?" Good question—even if I did ask it myself!!

We've already noted that nothing about the current sequence of events of the traditional wedding service is historically illegal. It does point up the fact that one can lop off the Betrothal Service from the rest of the rite and still preserve both its dignity and its meaning. Today, the inclusion of the ritual of betrothal in the wedding rite is not a legal requirement. If the wedding were broiled down to its lowest common denominator, the betrothal service *could* be totally eliminated. But, *if you do use the traditional wedding service, as do most people, let the entire occasion accurately reflect its historical meaning.* Otherwise, you will have a group of people gathered about you who are wanting to formulate a service that is both lovely and meaningful, but who stand not a ghost of a chance of accomplishing that goal without your knowledgeable contributions! Here's where the pedal meets the metal and where what one sees gives evidence to what one believes: With proper attention to what has heretofore been said, in the traditional wedding service the bride comes down the aisle on the LEFT arm of her father or escort, contrary to instructions in some etiquette books.

You are now surely among those who will understand the reasons for this strategy. When they come down to the front of the sanctuary her father will be standing between the bride and the groom, whose wife she shall shortly be. It does make a difference!! She, who now belongs to her father, is on the threshold of being "given away" to the one who will be her spouse. Upon hearing the question, "Who giveth this woman to be married to this man?" the father not only announces his intent but also grants his blessing upon the marriage about to take place. But then, if the bride's escort is not her father, that person should *not* be asked this question. It just does not fit into the context. No other relative or friend historically has the ownership of the bride and the authority to "give the bride away." Since this escort doesn't "own" her, he or she should simply escort the bride to the front of the sanctuary and then have a seat when the betrothal vows have been taken or before, clearing the way for the wedding part of the service to begin.

Incidentally, many brides of today who have been out of the nest for some time have made the distinct discovery that they no longer belong to their father or anyone else. As their own persons, they present themselves before the minister unescorted, or escorted by the groom or someone else, ready for the marriage service proper. They come prepared to give themselves away!

I can hear the moans of a lot of modern-thinking folks who experience an ugly distaste at the perception of the lovely lady of the hour being treated so much like a sack of potatoes, dominated by the major males in her family. It is not the author's purpose on this occasion to defend traditional ways of doing things. There are also meaningful contemporary marriage services that exhibit sound principles of worship. My main goal here is to urge folks to be true to history and to practice solid theology in worship. You certainly have the option to construct a different type of wedding service that blends with your own basic values, that displays the true meaning of marriage, and that fulfills the aims of true worship. *Whatever way you choose to do this rite, resolve to do it right!*

The Wedding Rite

The derivation of the wedding rite is lost in the shroud of history that somewhere along the way moved over the face of the earth. Most observers are aware of the fact that the verbiage of this sacred rite is not lifted from the hallowed pages of the Bible. It is true! In the Old Testament the nuptials ordinarily were described in their simplest, short-hand version. They cut right to the chase. They conserved words in the extreme in describing a wedding by condensing the whole series of marital events by saying that, upon completing the wedding feast, "the couple went into their tent and he went into her, and she bore him a child". That's pretty darned crude, but that's the way it is related in the Scriptures. Look at the story of the parents of Moses in Exodus 2 where the Book says, "Now a man from the house of Levi went and took to wife a daughter of Levi. The woman conceived and bore him a son." The biblical record is almost completely devoid of the descriptive details of any kind of rituals connected with marriage. It appears that the big emphasis was on the wedding feast, which—as has been said—was the form taken by the wedding in days of old. There is an occasion in the book of Ruth

(4:11–12) when a sort of benediction is connected with the wedding of Ruth and Boaz: "Then all the people who were at the gate, and all the elders, said 'We are witnesses. May the Lord make the woman, who is coming into your house, like Rachel and Leah, who together built up the house of Israel. May you prosper in Ephrathah and be renowned in Bethlehem; may your house be like the house of Perez, whom Tamar bore to Judah, because of the children that the Lord will give you by this young woman.' So Boaz took Ruth and she became his wife, and he went in to her, and the Lord gave her conception and she bore a son."

So we see that the wedding ceremony was an occasion of action rather than a time for taking possibly thoroughly forgettable vows and rituals. The real history of the service itself is unknown and sets us no pattern to follow. The thing of surpassing importance here is not the evolution of the ceremony itself but rather the meaning of that ceremony!

The Wedding Vows

We come now to the heart and soul of the wedding service. We recall that we enter the church on the occasion of the wedding service seeking the blessing of Almighty God upon the decision already made by the bride and groom. In His presence we express that decision in the form of vows. They are the essence of The Decision, now spoken before God as a plea for His approval and His blessing. Back during the 1980s, Church folks went through a phase when many young people often chose to compose their own wedding vows. Some of the homemade vows I heard back then were beautifully and lyrically expressed, but too often they missed the mark of capturing the biblical intent of the vows of fidelity to be taken by a bride and groom standing before the Lord God. So, the importance of the wedding occasion hinges on the vows then taken. There are several sets of vows in general use these days, all having a common meaning. I have prepared a list of those most frequently used to show to prospective couples as models for their use.

Here is my list:

a. _____, wilt thou have this_____(woman, man)
to be thy _____ (wife, husband),
and wilt thou pledge thy troth to _____(her, him)
in all love and honor, in all duty and service,
in all faith and tenderness, to live with ____(her, him),
and cherish ____(her, him),
according to God, in the holy bond of marriage?

*   *   *

b. I take you _____,
to be my _____(wife, husband) from this day forward,
to join with you and to share all that is to come,
and, with the help of Almighty God,
I promise to be faithful to you
as long as He gives us life together.

*   *   *

c. I, _____, take thee, _____,
to be my wedded _____(wife, husband)
to have and to hold, from this day forward,
for better, for worse, for richer, for poorer,
in sickness an in health, to love and to cherish,
Till death us do part, according to God's holy ordinance;
and thereto I pledge thee my faith.

*   *   *

d. I, _____, take thee, _____,
to be my wedded _____(wife, husband);
And I do promise and covenant;
Before God and these witnesses;
To be thy loving and faithful_____(wife, husband);
In plenty and in want; in joy and in sorrow;
In sickness and in health;
As long as we both shall live.

*   *   *

That's the list, incomplete as it is. You can see the main points of these vows. Each is a man-and-wife covenant pledging in the presence of Almighty God to be a life-long and faithful spouse when faced with any kind of life's conditions.

Remembering that the bride and groom make this vow to each other in the presence of Almighty God, see that they face one another, holding hands.

The couples each promise:

. . . to be a loving spouse
. . . to be faithful
. . . to honor their spouse
. . . to share all duty and service
. . . to practice these qualities unconditionally (in all eventualities)
. . . to fulfill these duties from now on.

Those last two parts of this marital covenant mark the areas of the frequent cave-ins. Under the threat of "no marital privileges without marriage," too many people enter marriage thinking that divorce presents an easy way out of the situation if things don't go smoothly. In fact, one gets the idea that when young couples encounter troubles, differences, or conflicts, they immediately bolt for the exit rather than hang in there and *do whatever needs to be done to solve the problems and make the marriage work.* We make that approach appear to be much too easy. It is most assuredly NOT easy. Death never is! Those who take this route out of marriage have to be ever conscious of having failed, of having taken vows before God in vain, and of being a party to the conscious execution of that "person" to which they gave birth by their marriage.

Reflecting further on the duties, the practices to which couples commit themselves in marriage, we verify the fact that these vows are not systematically laid out in the Scriptures. But they focus on the major themes spotlighted with force in such passages as Ephesians 5:21–32. Take a look at this passage, if you will.

Before commenting on what is found there, I need to say a little bit about what is *claimed* to be present (but is definitely not!) I don't know how many times I have heard sermons based on only a portion of this passage, as so many preachers have misrepresented the main point here as being, "Wives, be subject to your husbands." Friends, to quote only a portion of any passage while intentionally ignoring the totality of its meaning is taking the message out of its biblical context. This is a deceptive, dishonest, practice. This is *not* a Scriptural passage proclaiming the subservience of women and the superiority of men!

This passage is about husbands and wives *both* honoring their spouses. It is about their *sharing* all duty and service. The topic sentence is the first one: "Be subject to one another out of reverence for Christ." (v. 21). That's not a command for the women only, but it applies equally to husbands AND wives. The Bible here urges husbands AND wives to be subject to their spouses. It is very important for the clergy to grasp what is said here in order to be able graphically to explain it to the young couples who come for counseling before marriage. It will definitely be an issue when you discuss with them just what kind of marriage they want theirs to be. What you have to say on this issue will most surely make a huge difference in their marital perspective!

Much more could profitably be said on this subject. It serves partly to explain what is no longer a part of the wedding vows for wives: The promise to *love and obey* their husbands. That clause crept in there years ago by the hand of someone who undoubtedly misread this very passage. Shouldn't ever have been there!

The pastor and the couple can choose the vows to their satisfaction. As I have said, the vows each may be altered, but the essence of the covenant needs to be retained and respected.

The Analysis of the Wedding Service

It will be a simple matter for you to look back in this text to find a copy of the traditional marriage service transformed into a worship service. You can see there the simple elements that ought to comprise the wedding service, in addition to the vows, and their general order. Each such service ought to have . . .

a call to worship,
        prayers,
                a carefully-selected reading of the Word,
                a short homily,
                        the declaration of marriage,

the charge,
and the Benediction.

Recalling the real point of this service, ask the couple to face one another when speaking the vows. They're making the covenant with each other, seeking God's approval.

The posture of the couple during the benediction is generally a matter of personal preference. Some churches furnish kneeling benches. If so, it may be wise for them to kneel. Otherwise, you can take your choice between kneeling and standing. Neither way is disrespectful or wrong.

We have come down heavily on the meaning and position of *the benediction* at the conclusion of the marriage service. Not a prayer, the benediction marks the climactic conclusion of the wedding service, after which nothing further needs to be said or done, nor should it be!

Weddings, like any other types of worship service, can be concluded in a number of ways that are all quite different. We are currently discussing the benediction, but there are also the ascription and the closing prayer. Too many times lay and clergy alike tend to get these tools of worship confused.

The last of these, first: *The closing prayer,* as is true of all prayers, is always a human being calling upon, addressing the Almighty for any of a healthy list of reasons—praise, thanksgiving, petition, intercession, etc. In the case of corporate prayer, it is the leader (usually a pastor) verbalizing the thoughts and desires of those gathered and offering them to God . . . always saying "We ask . . ." instead of "I ask. . . ." The prayer is often practiced with the head bowed and the eyes closed, respectfully shutting out the distractions of the surrounding world as we focus on the "ear" of God . . . persons calling upon God!

The ascription, on the other hand, features a person attributing or assigning high praise to God, customarily quoting scripture as a transmitter. It is neither a prayer nor a benediction. When we ascribe blessing to God, we praise Him for always being the King of Kings and Lord of Lords. You are familiar with such an ascription as:

"And now unto Him who is able to keep you from
    stumbling,
And to present you before the glory of His Presence
    without blemish in exceeding joy,
To the only wise God, our Savior,
    through Jesus Christ our Lord,
Be glory, majesty, dominion, and power,
Before all time,
now and forevermore. Amen"
        (Jude 1:24–25)

The benediction is neither an ascription nor a prayer of any kind. The word is made up of two Latin words, bene-dictus, meaning "good word" or "blessing." Instead of depicting people addressing God, a benediction depicts God addressing people through the agency of His servant who is ordained so to do. It is the pronouncing of God's blessing upon people. It is the act of conveying God's blessing to others. It is written, "When God blesses us, He truly makes us blessed." To pronounce the Benediction is one of the two priestly functions which the minister is ordained to perform. Technically, anyone who leads a service can preach a sermon or lead a funeral or lead a prayer, but ordination as a Minister of the Word and the Sacraments empowers, authorizes one to impart God's blessing to the people. In the absence of a minister, anyone can be called upon to lead the closing prayer, but when present, a minister should be called upon to render the Benediction . . . an action done while the minister engages the members of the congregation eye to eye.

The pastor <u>conveys (not solicits!)</u> God's blessing to those congregated in that place and upon what the bride and groom have brought to and take away from this sacred hour through the medium of the Benediction, which is the essence of why we are in His house. It may be the only time and place during that whole week that the people can count on receiving a blessing instead of a condemnation in this wicked world. It says to the bride and groom: "You have taken these vows; now through this Divine Blessing, receive the strength to keep those vows forever."

Save the gauche and cutesy. "May I now present to you the new Mr. and Mrs. Joe Jones" until the reception. If said there at the wedding, it may get you a couple of "That's sweets" if indeed that fulfills your purpose for being there.

The definitive ending for the wedding service is the benediction. If you invite the people to stand for the benediction, that means that they will already be standing for the recessional of the wedding party. It seems appropriate for the pastor to suggest that the newlyweds seal their marriage with a kiss before gallantly recessing back down the aisle. (It also seems appropriate to advise the couple not to make a prolonged display of intimacy with this kiss.)

The wedding ceremony as we have described it is simple, meaningful, and ordinarily sufficient. However, **there are circumstances that seem to call for certain auxiliary wedding rituals**. One caution here is that the young couple may feel that what all has been planned for the wedding ceremony is somehow not enough. The danger is that too many additional rites will diversify the thrust of the occasion. I mention the following rites because they are not improper and because folks may need some guidance as to where to insert them into the service and as to how they should be done, for example, **The Unity Candle.**

This ritual is designed to make visible the idea that in marriage, two families become one . . . more specifically, two lives become one. A set of three candles is placed in the chancel area of the sanctuary, usually to the bride's left. The center candle, usually slightly higher or taller than the other two, is left unlit during the service.

Each of the other two candles, one standing for the bride and the other, the groom, is lit just prior to the beginning of the service by the fathers of the bride and the groom, by their four parents, or by one of the acolytes. Any of these ways is proper.

Then, during the service, just after the declaration of marriage, the pastor makes a brief introductory statement, the bride and groom move over to face the candles, simultaneously take a burning candle, light the center candle together, extinguish and replace to their holders the outside candles, and return to face the pastor.

The minister's commentary, or introductory statement, could go something like this:

"The Bible teaches that a wife is to subject herself
    to her husband.
And that likewise a husband is to subject himself
    to his wife—
Two lives divinely empowered to become one in
    marriage,
        while never ceasing to grow as individuals.
To symbolize this truth,
    Mr. and Mrs. Joe Jones
        will now light The Unity Candle."

Another beloved custom is **The Ritual of the Rose.**

A red rose is given by the bride or by both newlyweds to their respective mothers and possibly to their (grandmothers) as an expression of love and a salute to those who helped raise them. The flowers are placed on the altar or in the chancel area prior to the service. After the benediction the pastor hands the flower(s) to the bride (and groom) who gives it, along with a kiss on the cheek, to the proper person(s) just as they begin recessing. The ritual is usually done without dialogue.

The Inclusion of a Child (or Children) of a Former Marriage

Tragically, there are many too many divorces that take place after the birth of one or more children. Depending on the age of the child (or children), you may want to do different things in order to have them, not only feel but *be* an integral part of this occasion of melding two families into one. It is not uncommon for both the bride and the groom to have children who have reached the age of discretion. Especially older children need to be in favor of the marriage and ought to have a part in the proceedings. Many times the newlyweds have overlooked their children in the planning of a wedding, and these offspring often are not convinced that their parents are meant for each other, or are afraid that they will be thereafter neglected. Numbers of good marriages have come to an early conclusion because the children of a previous involvement were in fact NOT involved. This is a suggestion about ways to allow their children to say "We do, too!" when their parents are saying "I do!" (The wording will need to be slightly changed if there is but one offspring.) Rather than just spring the wedding on them, help them to know what is going to happen here and that this newly combined family is going to be theirs also! Their attitude and behavior will help to make it or break it.

Just prior to the wedding vows, ask the child(ren) to stand and take a vow expressing their approval of the wedding and their part in helping to make this new family successful. Obviously the parents should discuss these vows with the offspring *ahead of time* so that they are quite familiar with them.

This ritual could go something like this:

Vows That May Be Taken by the Children of the Bride and/or the Groom

In this marriage in which both bride and groom have been previously married to others, the involvement of the children is vital to all concerned. We, therefore, call upon the child(ren) of this couple, (list their names(s))_____ to stand and respond to these vows and promises:

1. Do you approve of the marriage of your parents now to take place in this sacred ceremony?
2. Will you pledge your consistent support to them in helping to make this new household a happy and successful one?
3. Will you contribute your gifts of patience, love, and encouragement so that both of them will experience your love for them?
4. Will you be open and honest with them both as they endeavor to form one united and harmonious family by the grace of Almighty God?

In the case of a very young child, the bride and groom

could at this point present the child with a little memento of the occasion. The rite, if a young daughter is included, could sound something like this: "This (ring) placed upon the finger of _____ (a daughter) symbolizes the mutual sharing of this love—and a family of three is born."

Now that we have scrutinized the make-up of the marriage ceremony, it is time to delve back into the process of planning the rehearsal. For the clergy, it should be obvious that this planning is a very important thing to do. More than one time I have attended a wedding rehearsal before which little or no planning was done. The confusion of the wedding party and the pastor was evident to one and all. What should take 45 minutes to an hour to do actually took 1 1/2 to 2 tiresome hours. The time invested working in the office beforehand would have produced great dividends at the rehearsal.

11

Planning the Wedding Service Rehearsal

The Purpose of the Rehearsal

This is a statement of personal preference. I never go through the entire wedding service, including solos, prayers, vows, and such. To do so would be excessively time consuming for one thing, and it would erase part of the element of spontaneity, which I think is an exciting and positive feature of the ceremony. The bride, the groom, and the Director should be informed as to the pastor's intention here just so that they will know what to expect.

The real purpose of the wedding rehearsal is to acquaint the wedding party with the surroundings, to acquaint everyone with their placement during the service, and to inform everybody about where to go and when to go there.

Some brides have been told that bad luck will come to the marriage if the bride personally participates in the pre-marital practices of the ceremony.

Oftentimes the pastor is the last one to learn that the bride entertains this superstition. It will be well and wise for the pastor to make it known here in the planning stage that you certainly expect both the bride and the groom to take part in the planning *and* rehearsal of the service. If she believes differently, she should bring it up for discussion at this point.

The Setting of the Rehearsal Time (with the Bride and Groom)

Customarily, the rehearsal is held at some time during the eve of the wedding. You will need to make every effort to plan around any other events scheduled for the wedding party. If they are intending to have a rehearsal dinner at a restaurant, they will need to make reservations there for a particular time.

Assuming a rehearsal dinner, you can schedule the rehearsal either before or after the dinner. Considering the work or travel schedules of the wedding party, do plan the rehearsal for a time when it is possible for them all to be there. It would be foolish to set up a rehearsal for 3 P.M. on a Friday when you know that some participants can't possibly be there until after 5 P.M. quitting time! If you can get your people to the church for rehearsal by 6 P.M. on Friday, then you could safely make a reservation at the restaurant for 7:30 P.M. Or reverse it and schedule the dinner for 6 P.M. and the rehearsal at 8 P.M. Incidentally, in over forty years of presiding over weddings, on not one single occasion has the entire wedding party been there ready to start the rehearsal at the prescribed hour! Sometimes no one was there at the church at the appointed hour except me. And I was on time every time! No worries. The entire nights were theirs anyway.

Atypical are the times when rehearsals cannot be held on the eve of the wedding service. Once I presided over a Saturday wedding service scheduled for 4 P.M. Several of the wedding party members couldn't be present for a Friday night rehearsal. Upon learning that there was to be a luncheon for the wedding party at noon on Saturday, I simply had them stop by the church an hour before the luncheon to rehearse. It worked like a charm.

This is a good opportunity to check out all activities related to this wedding which the pastor and/or your spouse is expected to attend, such as a party, the rehearsal dinner, etc. Many times brides and grooms have gotten their feelings hurt because the pastor didn't appear for an occasion where expected. They presumed the pastor knew that he/she was included. I never go to an occasion to which I have not received a definite invitation. To avoid unnecessary misunderstanding, it is wise at this stage of the planning to ask for help in filling out your calendar.

The Parental Blessing (Affirmation)

Called by any other name . . . we are talking about planning for the moment when the pastor asks the question, "Who gives this woman to be married to this man?"

Obviously, you can insert the names of the bride and groom here. But do not leave the answer to this question to chance!

Traditionally, the father of the bride provides the answer. Historically, his answer is "I do!" after which he gives his daughter a peck on the cheek, brings the bride and groom together, and then takes his seat beside the bride's mother. We repeat ourselves when we say that he is giving his daughter away and also is blessing the couple's union.

There are at least a couple of ways to modernize this transaction:

1. Most fathers these days answer, "Her mother and I!"
2. You may want to explore the possibility of having *both sets* of parents respond to the question by saying, "Joe's mother and father do!" and "Jane's mother and father do!"

Don't overlook the fact that you need to *take possession of the marriage license* by the time rehearsals take place, and to check its accuracy.

Before the beginning of rehearsals mention again the subject of "Who's in charge here?"

Back in an earlier chapter we answered and discussed this question. Ordinarily, the pastor is the one who is ultimately in charge of all worship services, including this one. It is most important that the bride, the bride's mother, and the person appointed as the wedding Director clearly understand this.

The Director needs to be given ahead of time an information sheet describing her job.

A pastor-Director consultation needs to be arranged prior to rehearsals . . . even if it is just 1/2 hour ahead of time.

The Conduct of the Actual Wedding Rehearsal

Be there on time! Then, there are a number of ways to get things started at rehearsals. Hopefully, these crude suggestions will help you.

The pastor first does these things to establish order and to set the tone:

Ask one and all (guests too!) to sit in the front rows on the same side of the sanctuary.

Introduce him/herself; welcome everyone; and remind the folks that their immediate purpose is to plan a worship service together.

Lead round robin introductions, starting with the bride and groom and the Director.

Briefly explain the nature of the service, as you have previously done with the bride and groom.

Note the things that you are NOT going to rehearse—solos, vows, prayers, etc.

Lead in prayer, asking a blessing upon the bride and groom, upon their marriage and upon your planning together of the wedding service.

The "Deployment" of the Wedding Party:

The term "deployment" refers to determining where the wedding party is to stand after they process down front in the sanctuary. Keep in mind that there is not a wrong way to do this. Traditionally, the pastor, the groom, the best man, the maid/matron-of-honor, the bride and her father occupy center stage down front. Some brides and grooms prefer to have all of the bridesmaids stand on the bride's left facing the pastor and the groomsmen, on the right. Others prefer for the ladies and the gentlemen of the wedding party to stand interspersed on both sides. It is purely a matter of personal preference.

The important thing to keep in mind is that the real purpose for the processional of the wedding party is to get them all down to the front of the sanctuary in good order where the action of the ceremony is to take place.

The Director should prove most helpful in bringing order to this situation so that the tall men and the tall women will exit together, and so on down the line and so that the flower girl and the ring bearer will have someone in the wedding party assigned to help them to know where to stand and when to leave the sanctuary at the time for the recessional.

After they get lined up, the wedding party should be prompted to face where the action is taking place at all times. This means that they should initially partially face the back of the hall, whence comes the bride—each at a 45-degree angle to the back of the church. When at last the bride and her father arrive down front, the others should re-position themselves to face where the rites are going to take place—at another 45-degree angle to the front of the sanctuary.

What you should have at this point is the father of the bride standing directly in front of the pastor with the bride and her maid/matron-of-honor on the pastor's right and the groom and his best man on his left, all flanked by the rest of the wedding party.

The Initial Walk-through of the Service

The pastor's introductory remarks should inform the wedding party just what is now going to happen. They should learn that the run-through of the service will be brief, concluding with practicing leaving the sanctuary before we practice making our entrance. It will help to remark that we can run through the service as many times as they wish, but that most wedding parties are comfortable with just a couple of run-throughs. Tell them not to be anxious about whether or not they are standing in exactly the right spot during the service. This will not be a precise military drill! The important thing is that each of them will be in position to see what is going on during the service. Besides, as the congregation is taking their seats following the invocation, you will have the opportunity to move them around, if needed.

At the conclusion of the betrothal portion of the service, the father of the bride steps back, (perhaps gives her a kiss on the cheek), takes the bride and groom by their arms, brings them together, and takes his seat beside the bride's mother.

The bride and groom then may follow the pastor, with the best man and the maid/matron of honor one step behind, up into the chancel area, or wherever the marriage portion of the service will take place. The pastor is at the center of the semi-circle there. The bride hands her bouquet to the maid/matron of honor.

Explain then what will take place there. Tell the bride and groom that their vows will be read slowly, and that if they miss a line of the vows, you will circle back and pick them up by repeating the missed line. They should expect you to ask them to face each other and join hands while taking their vows.

Concerning the ritual of the rings: When so requested, *the best man puts the ring that the bride will wear on the book held by the pastor.* If the ring should drop on the floor, designate THE BEST MAN to pick it up. The ring to be worn by the groom is supplied on request by the matron-of-honor. *If the groom's ring is dropped,* YOU (the pastor) should retrieve it.

If any of the ancillary or auxiliary rituals are used, talk about how they will be utilized.

Describe the conclusion of the service.

Now the pastor makes The Declaration of Marriage, reaching out and touching the newlyweds as you say the words, "Whomsoever God has joined together, let no human being put asunder!"

The Benediction

> . . . decide whether or not the bride and groom will kneel.
>
> . . . decide whether or not the congregation will be asked to stand.

Then, ask the newlyweds to rotate toward each other to face the exit and stop!

> The bride retrieves her bouquet from the maid-of-honor, who helps straighten her gown.
>
> The bride and groom gallantly exit, being given the full aisle before anyone else in the wedding party moves.

Then, at the rear of the sanctuary the Director stops the ushers as they recess, (perhaps the same ushers who brought in the mothers and grandmothers), and sends them back down the aisle to bring these same folks out.

Now you are ready to take it from the top! The entire wedding party lines up in the foyer or at the rear of the sanctuary, knowing where they are to stand when they move to the front of the sanctuary in the processional!

Repeat the initial walk-through of the service as many times as needed.

The Conclusion of Rehearsals

Get the Director to hold a brief usher's clinic.

Note: I attended a rather large wedding recently in a neighboring town. The groomsmen looked truly splendid in their formal, swallowtail coats. They obviously wanted to perform their duties with dignity and distinction, but it was evident that no one had given them any guidance about how to usher. At times their confusion was both painful and embarrassing.

Ask the ushers to line up prior to the wedding service along the left side of the aisle, inside of the sanctuary door.

a. Each mature female guest should be ushered on the *right* arm of the usher—regardless of which side she is to sit on—with her male companions and children following them.

b. Each unaccompanied male guest and children should be escorted (not ushered) down the aisle, and as they are seated, handed a bulletin, if such is available.

c. Unless otherwise instructed, the usher should ask, "How far down do you want to sit?," rather than asking, "Whose side do you want to sit on?," since the family and friends of the bride and groom are this day being made one!

d. As the women are taking their seats, the usher should gently assist them by taking their elbows. The usher then stands, with his back to the front of the hall and hesitates momentarily for the lady to be properly seated.

e. If the lady is to be seated on the usher's left, the usher stops just short of the pew she is to occupy, guides her by the elbow across in front of him to the seat, and again reverses to face the back of the church as he waits for her to be completely seated.

The ushering of the VIPs (mothers, grandmothers, etc.) is an additional project!

a. With the help of the bride, the Director selects the groomsmen who are to usher the VIPs (i.e. the mothers and grandmothers of the bride and groom, and possibly any other honored lady guests.)
b. Guests of the groom's family should be seated on the right as you enter and those of the bride's, on the left.
c. The bride's mother is the very last one to be seated before the beginning of the service and the very first to be ushered out after the service.

Let the Director select groomsmen to serve as acolytes.

a. The candles should be lit about fifteen to twenty minutes before the service begins—or prior to the arrival of the guests.
b. The acolytes are to carry the candle lighters with both hands, in a vertical position, with the flame about eye level.
c. If there are few candles to light, you may need only one acolyte. If two are used, they should go down the aisle side by side, start with the outside candles and work toward the middle, lighting them simultaneously.

d. When all candles are lit, the candle lighters should be extinguished and returned to the same position in which they were held as the acolytes entered. Then the acolytes turn to face back down the aisle and leave together.

After the service and the photo session, the candles are to be extinguished.
Plan the way the service will end.

a. Historically, after the recessional of the wedding party and the ushering out of the VIPs, the minister remains standing front and center holding in place the standing congregation. With a nod or some such gesture, the minister informs the congregation that the rites are finished and that they are free to leave.
b. More and more, the bride and groom are choosing to have the congregation escorted out, row by row. If this procedure is chosen, the Director should help select two groomsmen. After all is said and done, these two groomsmen will proceed down the aisle side by side, all the way to the front pew, turn around toward each other, and indicate to those occupying each pew that their time to exit is at hand.

c. If the post-wedding reception is to take place at a different site from that of the service, the wedding party often lines up after they recess and receives the congregation as they leave the sanctuary. This allows the guests who are not planning to attend the reception the opportunity to greet the bride and groom. It also allows the guests the luxury of being able to be on their way without having to wait for the photo session.

The planning of the post-service photo session.

a. I've not found a completely satisfactory way to arrange this occasion so that it will not dishonor either the wedding party or the guests, but the wedding party needs to know what is expected after the service.
b. It would please the crowd if the wedding party would go straight to the reception after the wedding in order to free the guests to go home early. But if they do this, the bride and groom invariably get to the photo session with wedding cake all over their faces and clothes. So, it may be the best idea to have the wedding party return immediately after the service to the sanctuary to get the picture taking over before coming to the reception.
c. The bride should meet with the photographer ahead of time to plan what shots can be taken before the service and what kinds of shots are desired later. A little pre-planning will make this occasion more efficient. Unless you do a little planning, there are some photographers who will take until a week from next Tuesday to do this job!

d. The bride should consider arranging for the guests to go through the refreshment line while the photo session is still in progress. This could preclude having a formal receiving line. When the newlyweds finally join the guests at the reception hall, perhaps the best man could proclaim their arrival by making a grand announcement, saying something like,
"Ladies and gentlemen . . . your attention, please! Please join me in greeting the new
Mr. and Mrs. Joe Jones!"

At the reception, the bride and groom could be toasted, preside over the ritual of cutting the wedding cake, and receive the good wishes of the guests in an informal manner.

It now occurs to me that there is a paucity of resources to guide us in preparing for those odd and awkward marital situations with which the clergy are occasionally faced. In this section I shall make a stab at trying to provide idea starters for those times when these types of weddings arise . . . and they do arise! These sample rites are the results of figments of experience, not of imagination!

The Making of a Marriage Contract with a Couple Whose Service of Marriage Has Already Taken Place at a Time or at a Place Not in Accord with the State Laws

<u>Situation:</u> The groom is a naval seaman who has a "window of opportunity" for the wedding, which has been planned for a time when his ship would be in port. The

bride has been married before and is assured by the clerk of court that her divorce decree will be in hand well within the allotted time. Plans for the wedding ceremony are made; announcements are sent out; the hall is reserved; all done in good time. There is only one problem: Due to a bureaucratic snafu the divorce decree is not in hand by the announced date . . . and, of course, a previously-wed person cannot be legally married again without first being officially divorced!

Decision time! It is not uncommon for a couple to elope, to have a civil marriage service, and later to have a wedding service performed by the Church. It's all legal!

Why not do it the other way around? After the church service held with no license from the state, another service may be held at a later date with divorce decree in hand, and a legal marriage contract is made. Here is a sample of such a service:

(At a gathering of at least two resident witnesses in the county in which the marriage license was issued, the marriage, already blessed by God in the Church, is legalized by observing the basic requirements of the State for the making of a contract as follows:)

The Minister Addresses the Entire Assemblage

The Greeting

"Ladies and gentlemen, this day too is the day the Lord has made; let us rejoice and be glad in it!"

The Invocation

"O Lord, Most Holy: Humbly and graciously we bow before You this day, assured of Your presence as we come. Guide us with Your Light, and fill us with Your Spirit, so that we may experience that sacred moment wherein You make two lives truly one. Father, we pray that You will bless _____ and _____ so that they may possess a union truly made in Heaven.

In the Name of Christ, we pray. Amen.

The Statement of Intentions (The Affirmation of the Meeting of the Minds)

Minister: We assemble in this place on this _____ th day of _____ of the year _____ for the sacred purpose of assuring that the marriage of _____ and _____ has the blessing of the State as well as the Church.

In affairs of the State, be it known that the parties to any contract need to be of one mind.

Without such an agreement, no covenant or contract can be deemed legal in the eyes of God or man.

So, _____ and _____, I now call upon each of you to give answer to this question about your intent.

Question: _____ and _____, do you now affirm before God and these witnesses that it is and has been your intention to be joined with one another in the sacred bonds of marriage this _____ th day of _____ of the year _____?

Answer: We do so affirm!

The Declaration of Covenant (or Agreement)

Then, now hear this: As one empowered so to do by the State of _____, I do hereby pronounce and declare that a true marriage has been made between _____ and _____ . . . duly noted and recorded this _____ th day of the month of _____ of the year _____.

The Benediction

Presiding Minister: _____
Witnesses: _____

_____

Date: _____

Note: Hopefully, the meaning and purpose of this ritual is clear. When you have occasion to use such a document, you may want to alter it to fit that situation. At least you will have something from which to vary. You will then use the data in The Declaration of Covenant to fill out the information asked for on the Marriage License, including the names of the two resident witnesses, and send it in to the clerk of court.

Case closed!

The Making of a Marriage Contract with a Couple Whose Wedding Service Takes Place Outside the Bounds of the County of License

Possible Situation: You have engaged in several pre-marital counseling sessions with a young couple who want to have an outdoor wedding in a relative's beautiful garden. Site unseen, you approve. The announcements have been mailed with the directions to the wedding site enclosed. At the eleventh hour, you discover that the site chosen for the wedding is located outside the bounds of the county where the bride and groom live and where they bought their marriage license. Of course, the marriage needs to be recorded as having taken place in the county where the license was purchased. The rapid approach of an impressively illegal situation brings instant panic!

<u>Possible Solution</u>: A couple in this predicament was planning to have their wedding reception in the home of the groom's parents, who did reside in the county where the license was purchased. So, the solution seemed to be simple: Since this wedding had already been blessed by the Lord in a church, they planned to have a second marriage rite, not a repeat of the first, back at his parents' house—this one to satisfy the need for a contract. The difference between this situation and the one in Sample #1 is that the family and friends here have just been to the wedding ceremony before coming back to town to the reception. So, something a little different was called for.

(<u>The setting</u>: It was arranged for all of the guests to return to the site of the reception prior to the arrival of the newlyweds. This gave them a chance to hear an explanation of what was to happen and why. So, the bride and groom were greeted as they entered the front door by the following brief ritual, which filled a serious purpose in a fun way.)

The Minister Addressing the Entire Assemblage

The Greeting

Hear ye! Hear ye, friends and neighbors! The honored couple of the day has arrived at the gates and indeed is crossing the threshold here at this very moment! Let this distinguished assembly joyfully greet them with a loud voice, "Olé!"

The Marriage Agreement

(The Minister, speaking to the bride and groom:) Know that your friends, neighbors and relatives assembled here cherish the opportunity to greet you at this high hour of _____ o'clock (am/pm) on this _____ day of ____in the year of our Lord _____, and to witness and affirm your being joined together as husband and wife this day!

_____ and _____, we call upon you both now to affirm in the presence of us all that you are joining together with one another in the true estate of marriage. Will you both affirm that statement?

(The BRIDE and GROOM respond:) Yes, we will!

The Declaration of the Agreement

Then, as one empowered so to do by the State of _____, I do pronounce and declare that you are now husband and wife together!

The Official Witness of the Agreement

And now, let the people here assembled show their approval by saying, "Hear, hear!"

The Conclusion (by the MINISTER)

Ladies and gentlemen, today we have witnessed the making of a new marriage! I now introduce to one and all the new MR. AND MRS. _____! And now, let the festivities begin!

*   *   *

So, now we have come to the end of our discussion about how to plan a wedding ceremony. Hopefully you can see the steps leading up to a wedding where tears could start to flow. Hopefully again there is sufficient material in this text to furnish additional assurance that you will experience many more *Tears of Joy* than *Tears of Sorrow!*

*   *   *

We will now turn our attention to the planning and make-up of that special worship service of the church—*the funeral service*—with the hope that we can make some of the same discoveries here.

*   *   *

PART THREE

The Funeral Service
A Celebration of the Resurrection

Introductory Remarks

So, now we change the focus of our attention from the special worship service employed to initiate a new married life to the special worship service used to initiate our life after death . . . the funeral. We have tried to emphasize the point that both the wedding service and the funeral service belong in essence to the Church. In the very first chapter I maintained that both of these services are generally treated as though they are more individually designed rites of passage than as true Church services of worship.

As we begin this section, then, we review something of the conclusions we drew that help define what we do and what we say on these special occasions. We said that a worship service is more than just a sacred rite; it is an exciting reflection of the Christian faith, an epiphany wherein God is revealing to us His grace. We also remarked with deep regret that these essential traits are seldom evident. Rather, the hallmark of both of these services as they currently are celebrated is blatant humanism . . . a characteristic about which we have the power to take effective corrective measures.

12

The Real Purpose of the Funeral Service

First, we envision what goes on within us when there is a death in the family, in the church family, or in the community. No matter whether or not that death is expected at the time it happens, when it comes, it has a chilling effect on the acquaintances of the deceased. Death is always an ineffable mystery that ever gives rise to fear. The unknown always does. *And there shall be tears!* It also evokes some profound questions, which sometimes are unutterable and often unanswerable. This is the state of things when, at funeral time, we respond to the clanging of the church bell and gather there with the family and friends. As we assemble, we do so *needing the steadying Hand of God to be laid upon us* to say, "Peace! Be still and know that I am God . . . even on a day such as this!"

What do we expect to happen at a funeral service? You have heard it said numbers of times that a *funeral service is for the living, not the dead!* None of us is going to disagree with that point of view. After all, in the twinkling of an eye, the dead have passed over from Here to There; they are no longer with us. Hopefully they are now in the full presence of the Living God. What is said at their funeral services, they will never hear. Only the living who attend these services will hear and see what happens. Therefore, we need obviously to bring the Good News, to address the needs, questions, desires of these living people during the funeral service. Sometimes this point seems to be forgotten. We experience real difficulty maintaining our focus on the reality of the funeral situation, addressing the status of the dead instead of that of the living! We are determined to recite a list of deeds done as if our recitation were going to insure the heavenly habitat of the deceased.

Our focus needs desperately to be readjusted. In the worst way we need to be reassured that God is present NOW. And we need answers to some pretty big basic questions, like:

The presence of Almighty God is evident when the world is full of life.

Where is He when we are zonked by death?

In a time of seeming disorder and chaos, who's in control?

If the Gospel is Good News, where is the Lord when we are immersed in bad news?

Is life here and now all that there is?

What happens at the death of one who has been morally inconsistent or even defective?

You can see that I am trying to bring direction to our thinking by advocating that at a funeral service the preacher needs to perceive and speak with force to these questions and needs of the people present—and this includes family and friends, *et al.* It is not a time for the sweet, soothing platitudes so prevalent in today's funeral services. We could ask the pastor on these occasions the question, "Just what do you have in mind?"

It is simply not a time for just eulogizing the deceased.

Another way to approach the subject is to perceive the

people gathering in the Lord's house for a funeral, asking, as they come, the question, *What does God have to say to me in an hour such as this?*

So . . . tell them! You will be speaking to the long-time resident of your neighborhood as well as the stranger you meet along the way. You will be re-telling the Good News, the Gospel of Jesus the Christ. Something of surpassing worth will be taking place! God *does* have something to say in this situation also!

This delivers us to the point to remember: *The centerpiece of the Christian funeral service is always the proclamation of Christ's victory over death and His promise that we shall share in that victory!* You can readily see that this description of the funeral's being a worship service and centering on the proclamation of Christ's Gift of Eternal Life renders the well-spoken eulogy of a person quite beside the point on this occasion. Otherwise, what you end up with is a "feel good" hour involving recitation of the supposed excellence of one person's life, the recounting of which will possibly eliminate the need of the saving work of Christ, which is not what a Christian funeral is about. *No matter how lengthy and impressive is the list of a person's accomplishments that person is still a sinner saved by God through grace.* That's the point here!

Many a funeral service utterly fails to make this fact clear and central. To focus on a person's good works to the utter neglect of the Good News of Christ is a mistake of drastic proportions. But this, in fact, is what takes place at a multitude of funeral services. We tend to give the people everything but what they really need and that for which they actually come to the Church. Lest this whole scenario seem impractical and unsatisfying, I'm going to include a complete funeral service in a few minutes. It will not be a perfect example of a funeral service, but it should give you something to think about and even to improve upon.

There is another cast to be put on what should happen at a Christian funeral service. *It should allow the family and friends to express their grief openly.* Notice the way that purpose is expressed: a funeral should ALLOW them to express their grief. To give expression to grief is neither required nor forbidden. It is most certainly permitted. I have been to a funeral service or two over the years where the leader appears to be satisfied only when everybody in the house is totally out of control . . . screaming and sobbing, sometimes absolutely distraught. It's literally a tear-jerker. "There shall be weeping and wailing and gnashing of teeth," said Jesus as He prophesied about the prospective events of Judgment Day. Such a show of deep emotion will arise from within because of a person's utter desperation when the type of person he has been finally comes to light. It has always struck me as being extremely cruel when the preacher's ultimate goal at the funeral service is to make people visibly disconsolate, to make them feel guilty, or lost, or hopeless, or more distressed than they would ever naturally be . . . and to make a public display out of it!

Where is compassion and comfort and fulfillment and forgiveness and hope here? It seems to me that the aim of this type of funeral service is far beneath the appropriate Christian target. A great feeling of power and control over people seems to be realized by those who bring about such a cruel and pathetic scene. Instead of merely allowing expressions of grief to well up from the inside, there are some ministers who forcefully try to induce it and who will defend the efficacy of this methodology. And there shall be tears of sorrow!

On the other hand, it is a loving and caring act to create

the kind of environment that embraces those who mourn and permits them to express it with impunity. "Comfort ye! Comfort ye my people, says the Lord."

Where should it be more free and more comforting to weep than in a place of worship, surrounded by family and friends who relate to your grief and who also weep with you?!

In this place you don't have to sob noisily. Neither do you have to feel embarrassed if the tears in profusion naturally come. We do not perceive a funeral in clinical terms, but a therapeutic environment is developed as the concern of our friends embraces those who mourn, and our grief is on the receiving end of the power-filled ministry of Christ.

A major purpose of a funeral service is to be a celebration of the Resurrection, which may naturally evoke tears of joy and tears of sorrow. Sometimes the twain do meet! This thought bears repetition.

Now, stand by because this next point will be more controversial than what has gone before: *The funeral service should not be viewed by the clergy purely as what is commonly described as an evangelistic opportunity.* Now, hear me out on this line of thought. I know this is not exactly what some preachers have been taught, but please be willing to take a close look at this viewpoint and keep it if it seems rational.

There are members of the clergy who view a funeral as a prime time to scare people out of Hell (or to scare Hell out of people, if that seems more realistic.) But consider what is being said here. I am definitely *not* suggesting that any pastor ever fail to seize the opportunity to proclaim Christ. *Pas du tout.* Just look at what has already been said earlier in this chapter. But consider the meaning of the term "evangelism," which really means "the in-bringing AND the up-building of the saints." Far too many of us focus our total attention on one of these two emphases (the first) to the neglect of the other. To some, being an evangelist is constantly to concentrate upon "bringing them in," on urging them to take that first step toward the Cross, of inviting and motivating those outside the Fold of the Kingdom to enter therein. This is certainly a very high priority of the Church. This we need to do constantly. I'm most certainly not denigrating that goal. BUT this is not the ONLY priority! What I am saying is that those who are present at the funeral—those who have already taken the first step and are already committed Christians—should be considered also, the up-building of the saints! These worshipers bear within them questions and fears and needs, as they ask, "What does the Lord have to say to me when death strikes close to home? Where is the Good News here?"

Take another penetrating look at the life of our Lord and be reminded of the ways He ministered to the people. He healed the sick, raised the dead, provided the way for the lost and the list goes on. At all those times He was ministering in the name of the Father, spreading His magnetic love . . . feeding the saints in many ways, all of which were (most often) done without requiring the attendees first to surrender to God unconditionally on the spot. And there is no record of Jesus' calculating how many souls were saved after any of His crusades. Nor are His ministries offered conditionally—that condition being that the people receiving His ministry necessarily accept membership in the Kingdom before receiving healing, wholeness, forgiveness, salvation! The Gospel embodied by Jesus won followers by appealing to their deep sense of need, by attracting them, by showing them the way out of their sin-filled predicament, *not* by herding or intimidating them.

A certain lady was well known as a good and faithful member of her church and her community. Her husband was well known in the community also, but not for anything connected with the Church. The only doors outside of his home that he darkened with consistency were those of the bars and night spots around town, but never those of the church. When he died, his widow came to the funeral service where she was surrounded by her good neighbors, all of whom also were wondering what God had to say to them at the time of the death of a well-known reprobate. What's the Good News here?

What was said at that graveside made them understand that their neighbor's husband was being judged that very day . . . but not by God!

The preacher began his remarks by saying, "We all know what's going to happen to our neighbor here. He's going to bust the gates of Hell wide open! (Can you believe that?!) It's too late for him. But for us, this is a reminder that you'd better get right with the Lord or you're gonna suffer the same fate." Then he took off at length on that note with the intention of frightening the whole crowd into a saving relationship with the Lord that very day. The minister appeared to be trying to *startle* the assembled neighbors into the Kingdom! Think of the disappointment of those who came that day just to comfort their newly widowed friend and to be comforted themselves. . . . Some of you will think that this pastor was justified in what he said that day. But I am maintaining that there is a different way—and a much better way—to proclaim the Gospel by the side of a grave. Give some consideration to it . . . to what evangelism really is, to what sort of message is suitable for a funeral; to what the Good News is in the worst of times.

Last if not least, part of the purpose served by the funeral is that *it is a memorial.* It is an aid to family and friends and a way for them to say "thanks for the memories." It is a chance for all to remember the gift of Life from

Christ, the contributions made by the deceased, and the nature of those gifts of faith and love handed down to the next generation. This is where some descriptive words of thanksgiving for the life of the deceased are appropriate, highlighting the faithfulness of his discipleship, and sympathizing with the terrible sense of loss harbored by the family. Just keep in mind that these words are *not* the main theme struck for and on this day.

Just this one additional thought along these lines. Say that during a certain week, one of the real saints in your congregation died. You told nothing but the truth when you presented a eulogy to her large family and friends gathered at the church. The very next week her scoundrel of a husband dies. You struggle unsuccessfully with putting together a similar eulogy for him. What in the world are you going to do and say? The children, family and friends clearly remember the vibrant re-telling a week before of the admirable deeds their mother had accomplished. Such a list does not exist for the father. His good family does not deserve to be subjected to a reminder of his wasted years. That's not Good News! Nor do they need to hear benevolent lies from the pulpit. This is just to point out that you can paint yourself into a corner by employing the structure of a eulogy at every funeral. It just does not work. It often results in the telling of thinly disguised lies, unsatisfying to all!

So, the complex purpose of a funeral service is to comfort and to strengthen people in their human grief and to minister by the proclamation of the gospel of Jesus the Christ to the pains, questions, and needs of those who are at the very moment moving through the very shadows of death.

13

A Crack in the Foundation
of the Funeral

Before delving headlong into the labor of constructing a funeral service, let us take note of the strange and unending efforts on the part of the clergy to justify their own presence in the pulpit at the time of a funeral service, by asking the question, "What qualifies us members of the clergy to address the families of the just deceased?"

This must be a legitimate question. Just think how often you have attended funerals where the ministers spent considerable time trying to testify to the assembled regarding their close relationship with the dearly departed (say, a man). The congregation there is subjected to a lengthy description of the supposed intimacy of the preacher's association with him and of the supreme value of that friendship. If, per chance, the preacher is unacquainted with the deceased, the pulpit is shrouded with great apologies for the man of the cloth not having known him. I speak here about this tendency because it is so prominent and not because it needs to be either said or heard.

I once knew a fellow who clashed with his new preacher from day one. He often talked about how they got off on the wrong foot with one another and just never did get on the right one. One day my neighbor died. At the funeral service I sat a few pews behind the family. Near the beginning of the service the preacher launched into a well-intentioned but fictional diatribe about how well he knew my departed neighbor, about how much he liked and admired him. I remember squirming uncomfortably in my pew during the service, as I knew that there was not a shred of truth in what he was saying. I knew that the family was even more acutely aware of the false claims being made from the pulpit. Of course, as his remarks continued, they led from "How much I admired and respected him" to a literally incredible eulogy. The preacher was saying, "I know from first-hand experience what a fine person he was, and that certainly gives me the authority to speak to you about his many good works."

You can see how that practice very quickly evolves into a dissertation on *salvation by works* that somehow has become the mainstay of many modern funeral services. Sometimes the preacher is unaware of the falsehoods he tells at a funeral. But the family of the departed one will certainly know. They have seen the good and the bad features about his character every day and have come to the funeral wondering about whether or not he qualified for Heaven (for which "many are called but few are chosen"). And they will—forever—be affected adversely by what was said during this funeral service. They will be far more disturbed than comforted by remarks carelessly exaggerating his flawlessness. To have blatant falsehoods stream forth from the pulpit at any time is simply a disappointing breach of trust. You just can't utilize that which is false as the basis for proclaiming that which is true and good. There has got to be a way to do it that is neither deceitful nor dishonest. Surely this is exactly what we have been talking about here. Maybe this whole situation has come about because many preachers don't know what else to say when there is a death in their midst. Maybe they are convinced that this is what the people want and need to hear. Maybe that is the type of oratory to which they themselves have most often been exposed when "death do us part."

Maybe the pastor didn't know the person who died, but hopefully he does know that the proper subject for this occasion is the Good News about the Christ.

So I ask again: Is it necessary for the preacher to know well the person who died in order to do an effective job with his funeral? Is the main purpose of a funeral service to recall the positive actions of the deceased with the hope that this will inspire the family and friends to overlook the negative ones? Surely we don't believe that the funeral message will change the mind of God sufficiently to influence anyone's Eternal Destination! The answer to these questions I am asking is a big, fat NO! Not if what we have described about a funeral earlier in this chapter is true.

14

A Sample Funeral Service

First, let's make two or three preliminary observations.

Let the funeral message *center on the saving act of Christ, not on the deceased.* That's just basic! The approach will seem different at first. It soon will let you know that you're doing something right!

By and large, a funeral service should be *brief.* You can't say everything on this occasion, but you can say some things very well!

Oftentimes a bereaved family is unnaturally dreading the funeral service. Their attention to what is said and done at the service is inversely proportional to the matters with which they are dealing internally. I often try to assure the family by telling them that the most valuable things that will happen to them during the time of worship may be the thoughts that they entertain in the course of their on-going grieving process. Such things are encouraged by the caring environment there. They may carry home a thought from the funeral meditation ... but certainly not a full-length theological thesis. It would be beneficial if the entire service did not last more than a half an hour.

Make the service *personal.* We have discussed the fact that the heart of the Christ-event ought to compose the centrality of the message on this occasion. That certainly does not mean that we ought to make it impersonal. After all, the reason why we assemble on this occasion is because of the death of a particular person without whose loss we would not be there. I attended the funeral of a friend some time ago and was a tad nonplussed by the fact that the man's name was never mentioned! There are numbers of ways that the name of the deceased can and should be mentioned. If the funeral were held in the sanctuary of the church, I customarily composed a bulletin for the occasion and included a page-long biographical sketch.

Sometimes I did the same thing for a graveside service. That certainly made the funeral hour more personal. Then, the message itself could include a brief personal history of the deceased, including what all he gave to and got from the church . . . a sort of personal testimony, all of which centered on the richness of the Gospel.

Consider the *music for the occasion*. You have probably already read the earlier chapter on music at weddings. The principles here are the same. This, too, is a worship service, meaning that the music centers on God's love for us. Any hymns or other music should be selected on that basis. The fact that a particular song was a favorite of the deceased is quite beside the point. He (she) is not going to hear it this day! That is not a sufficient reason for selecting it for this service. Actually, most music that I've heard at funerals has been anything but comforting. Most of it seems to be tear-jerkers rendered without adding anything positive to that hour. An Easter anthem would go well here. Have you ever witnessed, on film or in person, the funeral procession of a black congregation in New Orleans? On the way to the cemetery, the band plays a slow dirge with all its somberness and sadness. On the way back from the cemetery the mood has totally changed as the music blares forth in the celebration of the victory of another sinner who has arrived at his Eternal Destination.

There is an example to be followed here. We should expect all services to invite the participation of the worshipers in singing the great celebrative hymns of the Church and in the responsive readings of the Scriptures.

Some proper funeral services have *no intra-service music at all.* Just as is true of some proper weddings. Some time ago I attended the very impressive funeral service of a fellow clergyman which was made up entirely of very appropriate scripture readings and prayers. These were carefully selected biblical passages which consoled and comforted and said all that needed to be said to the family and to the friends. The service was short and impactful. Well done! The service to be included herewith is without intra-service music by the request of the family.

*   *   *

A Celebration of the Resurrection
In Loving Memory of
John Adam Smith
April 1, 1910—April 1, 2004
Thursday, April 4, 2004
2:00 P.M.

*   *   *

The Organ Prelude

The Greeting

My friends in Christ, we are gathered here on this day as a witness to the Resurrection of Jesus Christ and to give thanks to Almighty God for the earthly life and resurrection of John Adam Smith, whom God has now called to His Eternal Home. Where His people are, there His Church is. The Church is here! (. . . at a funeral home chapel!)

The Call to Worship

Jesus said, "I am the Resurrection and the Life.
He who believes in Me, even though he were dead,
    yet shall he live;
And whoever lives and believes in Me shall never die."

The Invocation and The Lord's Prayer

Eternal God, our Father, Who loves us each with an
    everlasting love:
We bow before You in faithful worship.
You are our Life and our Eternal Home
You are the Conqueror of Death, through our Lord Jesus
    Christ.
On this quiet *Thursday* afternoon following the death of
    our beloved
John Adam Smith make us most conscious of Your
    comforting nearness.
Touch us with Your Spirit that we may receive Your
    strength and wisdom.
Overshadow us with the glory of Your Presence, that we
    may be blessed by Your loving
care and may experience the Peace that passes all human
    understanding,
through Jesus Christ, Who taught us to pray, saying, "Our
    Father . . ."

Consolation from the Old Testament

Psalm 130
Psalm 46
Psalm 23

The Pastoral Prayer

The New Testament Lessons

1 Thessalonians 4:13–14
John 14:1–3; 27
Revelation 21:1–4
1 Corinthians 15:51–58

The Meditation

Today our minds methodically survey a tremendous amount of history.

Near the hour of sunrise on *Tuesday*, death came quickly and quietly to Mr. John Smith. As did we all, he received his life from God with no written instructions as to how to live it and no guarantee as to how long this earthly phase of it would last. Surely we cannot grieve because his life was too short . . . 94 marvelous years . . . nor can we wish for him additional mountains to climb nor rivers to cross. We gather here on this *Thursday* afternoon, not only to mourn Mr. Smith's death and to honor his memory, but also to celebrate the wonder of his life and his victory over death through the grace of our Lord Jesus Christ. God has sustained him through his 94 good years here, and now God has completed the cycle of life by reaching out to welcome him once for all unto Himself.

Today we can all sit back and ponder the great span of history and the long list of world changes that have been viewed by John Smith in the course of his lifetime. The world he entered and the world he left were so vastly different.

He grew up on a tobacco farm. In those days mules and wagons and sleds were the implements that bore the hand-picked tobacco from the fields to the barns and thence to market. No thermostats or automated furnaces controlled the curing processes.

Most of the streets in towns hereabouts were unpaved and lined, not with parking meters, but with hitching posts. Salesmen of high-tech gear were still touting the latest improvements in harnesses and brute-tough wagons.

History was in the making. In 1900 Wilbur and Orville Wright conducted their first experiment with gliders at Kitty Hawk, NC. After much laboratory work, they returned from Ohio to Kitty Hawk in December of 1903 to make the world's very first power flight—120 feet in just twelve seconds!

As he negotiated his way down the corridors of time, Mr. Smith served as a fine role model for us as he put his life in the hands of the Lord. The thoughts set down in this little poem by D.C. Gordon seem to express those of Mr. Smith:

In His Hand

I shall not fear to walk alone
If before me walks my God;
I shall gladly follow where e'er He leads.
My path is the one He trod.

I shall not hesitate to climb
The mountains, which now I see;
Because I remember how—long ago
My Christ climbed Calvary.

I cannot see the end of my path,
I cannot understand;
But in my heart live peace and joy—
My life is in His hand!

(*Note:* The author thanks the estate of the late D. C. Gordon for permission to reproduce his poem above.)

The moon back then was like a hunk of blue-green cheese, hanging mysteriously out there in space in a site which people could see but never touch.

When John Smith was born, the 26th U.S. president was in office, President Theodore Roosevelt. We fast-forward the years to find the 45th president now in office.

Yes, the world of today is a different place, changed by air and space travel, and also by a myriad of medical discoveries, the communication revolution, and even by a half-dozen major wars.

The local church had evolved much too. In 1937, when Mr. Smith and his wife joined Central Church, the people here worshiped in a small frame building out in the country right beside the pastor's house. It had no indoor plumbing, no organ, no carpeting and no pastor! In the intervening years Mr. Smith served this church in a variety of ways. He was an elder and a trustee for a number of years. A couple of years after joining this church, he began to teach the Men's church school class and taught it continuously until his retirement from that post two years go.

During that time the present brick sanctuary and Christian Education Building were erected. Faith speaking to faith—he contributed greatly to the growth of this church.

Again, we are reminded that we certainly have no grief at all concerning the length of his life, for at the end of a very long full lifetime, death has come from God to heal that which cannot be healed in this world, to dismiss all pain and infirmities, to open opportunities that have been closed here, to restore youth like the eagle's, and to fulfill the dream of a lifetime for all Christian people everywhere: the personal discovery of the truth of the Gospel of Jesus Christ, Who said, "I will come again and receive you unto Myself that where I am, you may be also." (John 14:3)

So now, this specifically is what you and I have come today to hear—the answer to this question: "When someone in our family or our community dies, what does God have to say to us who are still here? Where is the Good News now?"

The Good News is that Almighty God makes promises to His people, and that through Jesus Christ, God keeps those promises . . . to <u>Mr. Smith</u> and to us all!

We can now see death to be for us a very inviting door—the ONLY door out of this life and into Life Eternal. Let us, therefore, not anger ourselves at death!

The Bible speaks the comforting truth when it says to us, "I have loved you with an everlasting love says the Lord, your God."

And so, this day <u>Mr. John Smith</u> is the recipient of that love as God bears him up in those everlasting arms into the fullness of His presence for all Eternity. God gives us the uplifting joy of knowing that <u>Mr. Smith</u> has reached the destination sought by us all! Thus, we Christians can affirm that "we mourn not as those who have no hope," and God moves us to rejoice at the superlative truth that he has indeed arrived at the Ultimate Destination, that he knows now about being in the full presence of the living God, Whom for so many years he has seen only as in a mirror . . . dimly.

Hear now the Good News of Christ as it rings out like a bell to us this day. It was He Who said, "If you will just believe in Me, I will come again and receive you unto Myself that where I am, you may also be"—and He has done just that . . . to our loved one!

In the name of Christ, I implore you *to believe that Good News*—that we may in faith celebrate together—for Mr. Smith and for ourselves, as we say, *"Thanks be to God, Who gives us the victory through our Lord Jesus Christ!"* Amen.

The Prayer of Dedication

The Benediction

The Organ Postlude

*   *   *

Comments on this Funeral Meditation

The service in the sanctuary is brought to a conclusion with the benediction, as is the one at the cemetery. The reason for this is that there will always be friends who will attend only the service in the sanctuary (if that is where it is held) and those who will attend only the graveside service. Therefore, it is proper to consider each one as a separate, complete service. It is not really appropriate for the clergyman to say at the end of the service in the sanctuary, "This service will be continued at the cemetery." Each service has a different purpose and is complete in itself. The graveside service is very brief, is made up of words of committal, relevant scripture and prayer. It brings home to family and friends the closure, the finality of the death that has taken place. The benediction is the proper conclusion for each of these two services, with the family included when all are invited to stand at the end.

Just a little sidebar: Incidentally, it seems to be a custom at the conclusion of the graveside service for the pastor to pass down the rows of the family members, whispering to each one some inaudible words of inspiration and encouragement. I have avoided that practice. I think the short service ending with the benediction, includes everything that needs to be said at that time. When I visit with the family at their home prior to the service, I try to review what will take place at the church and at the cemetery. I tell them (and the funeral director, too!) that I will simply invite the family to join others as they stand for the benediction at the conclusion of each service, and then I shall step over toward the automobiles as the funeral director indicates to them that it is time to depart. They will have the opportunity to greet people before leaving the area if that is their desire.

15

Selecting the Funeral Service Site

A little something to ponder: There certainly ought to be a difference between the funeral service for a faithful Christian and that for all others. The site of that service may spell that difference, but not necessarily.

When I visited the homes of members right after a death had occurred, I often was invited to make a recommendation as to where the funeral should be held. Usually *the church sanctuary would be my preference.* However, I have never tried to say to a family that a funeral MUST be held in the church in order for it to be a Christian service.

There are all kinds of advantages to staging a funeral service for a faithful member in the church sanctuary. The family comes into a familiar environment devoted to worship, which is very comforting to all. Included in this familiar scene are the choir and the pastor. There is, of course, a form of Christian witness in choosing the church as the site of one's final rites.

Lately, more and more families are choosing to have the service in a funeral home chapel. In some ways this site is easier for folks. In case there are people coming from out of town just to attend the one service, or if some of the family or friends are elderly and don't drive at night, it may be wise to plan for the visitation at the funeral home an hour before the service is scheduled. If the service is planned for a week day, either morning or afternoon, it will omit some working people who would ordinarily choose to be at your side at a time like this. Most funeral homes are well supplied with lists of available choristers and musicians who are familiar with the repertoire. Another advantage of utilizing a funeral home chapel is that it requires less lifting and moving of the casket, all of which can be done by the staff of the funeral home.

As a matter of protocol, at the very beginning of a service held in a funeral home chapel, *I have always declared that chapel to be a church* by saying something like this: "The church is not just a building; it is God's people wherever they are gathered in His name. Today God's people are gathered here. Surely the Lord is in this place."

With the time and date for the funeral service having been set, depart, assuring the family that you will be in and out of their home between then and the funeral time.

The other place where funerals are sometimes held is *by the side of the grave.* I have to confess that the appropriateness of these last two funeral sites has evolved for me in a very positive way. There was a time when I thought that family members who chose to have their parents' funeral service either at the funeral home or beside the open grave were treating an important occasion of the Church in a rather cavalier fashion. I learned through my own experience that this was not necessarily the case.

When the time came for me to arrange for the final rites for my own mother, who was a very active church member her entire life, I resided in another state and I needed things to be efficiently planned. As my mother was advanced in years, and a lot of her friends were getting up there, too, the less any of them had to venture out of the house, particularly at night, the better. So, the notice in the newspaper informed folks that the service would be held at the cemetery at 11 A.M. and that the family would receive visitors *at the cemetery* one hour prior to the service.

It worked marvelously well. And the graveside service contained all the elements that the services in the church would have featured—even including hymns, which the pastor lined out, and the people actually sang!

I need only to mention here the occasions when a funeral service is held for *a person whose body has been cremated.* Time and again questions arise about whether or not there is anything in the Bible forbidding the act of cremation. The answer is, "No, there is not!" There are a number of reasons why a family would request cremation. It could be because of environmental considerations, or the disfigurement (by an illness or by an auto accident) of the person for whom the funeral was planned, or various other personal reasons. (Think of battlefield deaths). It should be noted *that you do not have to have a body present in order to have a funeral.* Nevertheless, you can certainly have a funeral service for a person who has been cremated. You can hold such a service at a church or at a funeral home chapel.

In addition, it may be necessary to compose a special worship service to carry out the wishes of the deceased person to have the ashes spread over a certain piece of real estate or body of water. My point here is not to recommend one site over others, but to affirm that a funeral may be properly held in a church sanctuary, a funeral home chapel, by the side of a grave, or at any other site of choice, as long as it is a service of worship and that the families involved understand what is done.

16

Preparation for a Funeral Service

Publicity items concerning death and funeral services should be put in the church newsletter from time to time, particularly when no funeral is on the immediate docket. One such item could be an account of what to do if death should occur at their houses. Already mentioned is the proposal to ask your ruling board to form a policy concerning funerals, even including a list of which relatives to whom the church will send flowers when there is a death in the church family. Another would be a description of the proper elements of worship for a funeral service. Such matters come under the heading of "long range planning for funerals."

News of the death of a church member may come to the pastor by a variety of routes—a call from a member of the person's family, from the hospital, from the police, from a representative of a funeral home—or the pastor may be on hand when death happens, particularly if the person has been gravely ill. If the death is expected, the pastor often has a chance to think about the funeral service ahead of time, perhaps even to talk about it with the patient or with the family, although most families seldom relish such an opportunity.

The important thing to remember is to go immediately when you get the news of a church member's death! When the death is unexpected, going to where the family is gathered is not all that appealing, but it is likely the place where your presence is more needed than any other place you could be at that time. The minister is expected to put his (her) personal objections and possible excuses out of mind and go!

Your apparel and looks are unimportant. Your thoughts about what to say when you get into the presence of the family are certainly a part of your preparation. But some of the most disappointing actions of the clergy during the advent of a tragic death occur when the clergy person shows up spouting fail-safe Scripture verses chosen in a vacuum. Many's the clergy-person who absents himself from such a troublesome situation as this by seizing upon the excuse of "not knowing what to say."

Of course you don't know what to say! If you think you do, you're probably mistaken! Your initial words are seldom that important anyway. But that's part of your job. What is important is that you are there . . . that you have a hug to share with other concerned mourners, and that someone folks depend on is on hand with some necessary support. Your prayerful attitude will usually inspire you to sense the mood of the family, and that will be reflected in your brief and unrehearsed prayer. Down the road apiece somebody will remember that you came when you were sorely needed and that you spoke words of worth that said something to them, like, "This is a very tough night, but we're gonna make it . . . with the Lord's help!"

And if you happen to be away from your desk when you get the news, you still need to call the family to express your stunned regrets and to let them know when to expect to see you.

The first visit with the family after a death may not naturally lead to a discussion of the up-coming funeral service, although it is usually true that the sooner this conversation takes place, the better it is for all concerned. By necessity you sometimes will need to feel your way along and try to sense the proper thing to do or say. For most families this conversation is spanking new territory. And it just may be that they have a relative or a former pastor whom they would like to invite to lead or to participate in this service. If they mention such an idea, it would be gracious for you to offer to contact that person and to get back to them with the result of your call. Making that contact also will give you the opportunity to detail what portion of the service you want the guest minister to take. If the family says nothing about what they expect, it may be wise for you not to assume that you will be asked to accept the responsibility for the entire service. If such is the case, it would be helpful for you to say something like, "Whatever I can do to help, I'll certainly be pleased to do it."

If you sense that the family is expecting you to preside over the service, since you are the only pastor the family has, then it would be helpful for you to assume the initiative by saying something like, "If you all have a special poem, or a hymn or a scripture passage you particularly want included in the service, just let me know; otherwise, I will take care of the service the best way I know how." From what has been said earlier in this book, you will know that this puts the responsibility for the service where it belongs: on the Church and not on the family.

Think about what your role as pastor of the family should be at a time like this. Terminate this visit after a suitable time—which means to be intentional about not staying too long—ending with a scripture reading and a brief prayer. Allow the family and neighbors to discover in your absence the roles that they can helpfully fill. As you depart, let them know that you will be in and out of their house several times prior to the funeral service just to see how things are going.

I realize that my usual routine connected with a funeral is rather time-consuming. I depend on conversations with the family to inform my comments to be made in the bulletin and in the message. I listen with care to the types of things the family members wish to remember with relish about the one who has died. They will hear some of those things reflected later in the funeral service.

The pastor will need to inform the family and the funeral director that he (or she) is coming by the house to make a pastoral call <u>on the day of the funeral about half an hour before the time of the service</u> just to see how everybody is doing. I know that most pastors don't do this anymore. But I happen to think that this is a very important thing to do. The family needs to know exactly what to expect that day. Some people harbor exaggerated dread of the events surrounding the funeral, and often with good reason. They have heard horror stories about the shouting and screaming that goes on at some funerals. If there are children present, they will need some strong words of assurance. Even some grown-ups will appreciate this pre-service visit, maybe for the same reasons also.

When the household is assembled, you may give them copies of the funeral bulletin (if you print one) to read privately. Inform them that nothing scary or surprising will happen today. Those things are in the past. The service will be something like a ceremony retiring the jersey of a beloved athlete whose physical prowess they will remember joyously while at the same time experiencing the nostalgia of realizing that they will no longer be able to watch him perform. They may see or have some tears during the service, which is okay. Then, tell them what to expect at the church and at the cemetery. Have a short prayer before leaving and assure them that you will be right there to greet them when they arrive at the church, whether by the funeral home's courtesy car or their own family vehicles.

Again, the size of the city and the travel distances involved may not allow the inclusion of all things mentioned. If it is workable, the entire occasion will be the better for it.

17

The Church: Funerals and Fraternal Organizations

There are a variety of viewpoints concerning the participation of fraternal organizations in funeral services along with the Church. Several organizations have very old and very meaningful rituals that they perform beside the graves of their recently-deceased members. Prominent among them are the Masons and the Odd Fellows. When a Mason or an Odd Fellow who is a church member dies, a representative of that organization usually contacts the church office to inform the pastor that a family member has requested that their organization perform their graveside rites. Then, the caller usually requests that the pastor have the benediction at the conclusion of their ritual. The Masons, as a matter of fact, usually expect to preside over everything that happens at the gravesite.

Generally, there are no Church rules or guidelines dictating how we are to respond to such requests. So, we may survey our options and act as we may deem wise. Here's what works for me:

a. In the case of a call from the Masons, if the family has asked for the Masonic Rites, there is really no alternative but to accept it. After the service in the church, I then go with the funeral procession from the church to the cemetery and mingle with the family and friends without commenting upon what all is being done. I do not participate at all in the non-church rites at the gravesite, which means that I advise them to have a closing prayer rather than to call on me for the benediction.

b. When other groups are to take part in the graveside service, I simply tell them that I will fulfill the prescribed service of the Church, concluding with the benediction, after which I will step aside, yielding the floor to them.

c. It would be wise for you to contact the various fraternal organizations in your town and talk to them about whether or not they have graveside rites for their members and what role the local pastor is expected to take. Your compiling a file on such matters would be a helpful thing to do.

d. One should not read into these actions any personal or professional animosity toward these or any other organizations. Certainly we must treat them with the greatest respect and kindness. My actions should only be construed as an attempt to keep the doings of the Church utterly separate from those of any groups and organizations. They are not equal. Try that on for size. If it fits, wear it!

A Word about the Role of Funeral Directors Needs to Be Inserted Somewhere Along in Here

My basic statement about funeral directors is exceedingly complimentary! The people I have met in that business have generally been very professional, very efficient, and very effective—in a word, excellent people! They just do what they do well. It is vital that you believe I am telling you exactly what I think, because down the page a piece I'm going to share with you the things concerning funerals that I think ought to be done differently.

The funeral directors and their staff come to your home, to the hospital, or wherever death has occurred to take possession of the body, and quickly and quietly guide you through the steps you now need to take. They help to produce a write-up for the newspapers and to arrange for the funeral service and the burial. They welcome the pastor into the conversation and thereby cut down on the number of phone calls necessary to check and see what times and dates are open for the events ahead. They will help the bereaved family by preparing the body for burial, by discovering how many copies of the death certificate will be needed, and who needs to get one. They will help the family in selecting a casket, and generally advise and direct the proceedings during the entire experience.

Now, many times disagreements between funeral directors and the clergy occur because the clergy has not recognized and faced the fact that <u>the funeral directors in their own eyes are in charge of the entire funeral service</u> no matter whether the service takes place in the church, in the funeral home chapel, or by the side of the grave. They are the ones who meet with the family to plan the particulars of the service; they are the ones who tell the family what time they need to leave home for the service, greet and usher them to the service site, and take charge of their exit and their return home. Note that a member of the funeral home staff most often is the one who contacts the ministers, often informs them that a death has taken place, directs the service, including telling the minister when to have the congregation to rise and when to sit, signaling the minister when to start the graveside service, and ushering the family back to the vehicles afterward. Before they all depart from the cemetery, the funeral director (quite significantly) will extend a hand—acting as the host in charge of the en-

142

tire affair—and express his thanks to the minister for helping them with the service.

You should recognize that, in addition to the duties mentioned above, <u>the funeral home staff is generally prepared to do whatever else has to be done to make the funeral service work, particularly whatever no one else will do,</u> and that could include a peculiar laundry list of chores. Let me give you some examples of what I'm talking about. There are a number of small churches out in the boondocks around the little town where I used to live, some of which were abandoned or only housed worship services once a month. I remember looking at the contents of a funeral home van, which they routinely dispatched to these little churches several hours before a scheduled funeral. The nature of its contents was absolutely astounding. There was a ring of skeleton keys just in case no one from the church was there to open the building. There was a big box of kindling wood in case the building was unheated. Up against the front seat was a large box of candles if there happened to be no light in the church. And there was a stack of old-time hymnbooks in case they were needed.

Few folks ever realized all that the staff of that funeral home had to do to be prepared for every possible emergency. Historically the task ably done by the funeral home staff has evolved into its present complex form as a product of their willingness to do whatever is necessary to make a funeral work and to make it appealing to their potential clients. <u>Their job description has been determined by whatever has fallen into their laps</u> through the years. There are some cases and places where the funeral home finds itself between a rock and a hard place. They are ever desirous of acting in behalf of their customers and yet acting also for their own good. Their health and welfare is dependent on their volume of business. Among other courtesies, they offer their facilities for visitation as they deal with the grieving family. Until fairly recently it has been considered unethical for funeral homes to advertise, but hosting a visitation gives them a golden opportunity to show off their plush facilities and to display their artistry at preparing the body for burial. These things certainly enhance their reputation and promote their business, and they also provide a very helpful service to people in need.

Now, let this serve as a reminder that the staff of the funeral home are basically merchants more than anything else. Always be aware that they sell caskets, and other merchandise.

Keep in mind the kind of funeral arrangements that you favor and do not allow yourself to be distracted. Do not rush to assume that the selection of a costly casket will be the final complimentary act you can do for your departed loved one. That opportunity presents itself when your loved one is still alive! When my dad died, I was ushered into the selection room of the funeral home to choose a casket. I felt like they were all much too expensive. It occurred to me that I was a victim of whatever that funeral home had in stock at that particular time. Of course, it is not likely that I would amble around to another funeral home to compare their stock. I'm certain that the duty funeral director where I was trying to do business thought I was a loose wire when I pointed to one of the least expensive caskets and asked, "Sir, where is the box that that one came in?" If he had told me that the box was in the back room, I would have chosen it in a heartbeat!

Most churches now own a pall, which is a decorative cover with Christian symbols on it to be placed over the casket during the visitation as well as during the service. It makes all caskets look the same, whether they are made out of solid gold or plastic or balsa wood. Most people (despite inexperience in this matter), feel that the cheapest casket is the best, saving a larger sum of money to be used for the survivors.

While we're talking about funeral prices, you need to inquire about the cost of cremation, which doesn't involve embalming or a casket or grave clothes. Since I've been out and about, federal regulations now require funeral homes to list the prices of all their services. When last I arranged a family funeral, the director showed me the list of the activities that they provided with no prices shown. The list included such things as a visitation room, a family limousine, thank-you notes, an organist, grave clothes, etc. From this list I chose four of them as the ones we wanted and asked how much these would cost. His answer: "Oh, some of these items cost the same as all of them." My response: "Well, sir, in that case, we'll take everything you offer." And we did!

These remarks are to suggest that if you do not think about the cost of things concerning a funeral, you'll allow yourself to spend much more than you can afford. Most folks are really not prepared to make these kinds of decisions or possibly to bargain at the time of death. Maybe their pastor will be their most likely source of help and support in this process.

My Preferred Funeral Arrangements

There are some few basic procedures that I would change, which would have the effect of putting the Church at the center of the funeral activities, and which would probably gain the approval of most of its members. The funeral home would still furnish the transportation for, and the care of the body. Also, they would continue to furnish write-ups to the newspaper, and funeral counseling—such as how many copies of the death certificate to get and where to send them.

Visitation would be held *in the church fellowship hall rather than in the funeral home,* possibly the night before the funeral. The ladies of the church would be asked to act as hostesses and serve coffee, punch, and cookies.

On the day of the funeral service, the pastor would still visit the family and have prayers. *The church officers, not the funeral home staff, would meet the family when they arrive at the church, and some of them would usher this family into and out of the sanctuary.* The custom followed by a number of large churches has the family gather before the service in the church parlor and then be escorted into the sanctuary by the funeral home staff! Why?! It would surely be much more comforting to the family for them to be greeted at the church and seated by people familiar to them—the church officers—rather than strangers.

The pastor would greet the members of the family as they exit the service to enter their automobiles just to check and see if everyone is okay. The pastor also would greet the family when they arrive at the cemetery and escort them and the casket to the gravesite.

This procedure would also have the effect of establishing the Church as being firmly in charge of the funeral services with the funeral home staff providing strong support. (Of course, the down side of that situation would be that the church officers would have to be trained in funeral procedure and would have to show up for funerals!)

The casket would remain closed at all times, except possibly for members of the immediate family. We tend to make the body present and the casket open as the foci of our attention in the same way that we do at a wedding with "the bride all dressed in white." In both instances it skews the purpose of the worship service for which we assemble. Anyway, viewing the body is a distinctly pagan practice injected somewhere along the way into the system of the Chrisitan church. My constant suggestion that families leave the casket closed and that the body be buried with only the family present fifteen minutes before the funeral service has generally been met with great disdain. Most folks have expressed the concern that out-of-town family members particularly would be furious if not allowed to view the body. Surely the beliefs and needs of the primary family should receive preferential treatment. The idea that the body is the house this deceased person used to live in and is now vacant is a hard sell!

These funeral ideals could be realized only with great difficulty, particularly if the service is held on a weekday when the members of the church are "on the clock" at their work places. That makes a group of church officers hard to assemble for the services. You can plainly see why these suggested changes in procedures are generally opposed by professionals of the funeral business. However, I would like to see them implemented. It would clarify the lines of responsibility tremendously and would magnify the warmth and comfort of the families involved.

18

After the Funeral Service

The pastor should lead or escort the family from the gravesite back to the vicinity of the cars where they may choose to greet friends.

The old country boy in me shows up here again! It provides somewhat of a closure to the day if the pastor follows the family home from the cemetery—not necessarily to enter their house, but simply to say that he/she hopes the day has gone well and that he/she will drop around again to see them very soon. The family is invited to call the church if a question or need arises in the meantime.

A recent funeral ritual these days is for the Women of the Church (or some other group) to provide a meal for the family after the funeral service and often to include all the guests. This is a good occasion for the pastor to mix further with the family to express the hope that the services and indeed the day have gone tolerably well.

In another day or so the pastor may drop by the house just to see how the family is dealing with everything and whether or not they need any additional thing. Leaving them a copy of the funeral meditation may be a helpful thing for the pastor to do.

It would be a supportive move for the pastor to visit their house again briefly after a month or less. An obit or notice of some kind should be published in the next monthly church newsletter. Discuss the funeral with your ruling board to see if they register any suggestions for improvement of future funeral services.

One further mention of MONEY!

Whatever other truths can be uttered about money, it is the most frequent spawning ground of vicious conflict, particularly within the family of survivors. Some of this may show up at the time of the making of funeral plans.

Example: A parent dies, and the child living in the same town begins making funeral arrangements according to his own thoughts about the occasion. From out of town come other siblings with other ideas, most about how much of OUR money should be spent . . . . and the will has yet to be read! Already the battle lines are drawn about how the children are going to divide the inheritance, which by "natural rights" becomes totally theirs upon their parent's death. They do the math, and, if there are four siblings, each figures that one fourth of their late parent's property is his or hers. They are ready and willing to fight for it!

I introduce this subject in this way because of the definite probability of your being included, like it or not, in a pertinent family discussion beside the funeral bier of their parent. It will be well if you have given the matter some forethought. **I stress here the importance of every adult having a will,** and I emphasize a certain viewpoint. Let's get on with that second point:

Example: The father of the clan dies. To whom does his property really belong? The answer to that question is that it belongs **to him and to his estate!** It does NOT belong to any or all of his children. He can do whatever he wants

to do with it . . . now or later (through his will). If he so desires, he can leave every bit of it to some charity or to the
Church of What's Happening Now and none to his children. It is simply wrong for children (survivors) to think
that they have an inalienable right to claim any or all of
their parent's property.

So, this is just to be assured that you have a little moti-
vation to consider the subject of inheritance and to gain
some well-founded perspective of it.

*   *   *

PART FOUR

After All Is Said and Done . . .

19

Final Thoughts

So, now, our quick survey of the health and welfare of weddings and funerals as special worship services of the Church is at an end. I hope and pray that the discoveries promised in the introduction to this little book have been explicitly fulfilled during the chapters that followed. As stated there, the main purpose of this grand undertaking was to give you something worthy to think about rather than to try to enlist your support for a particular body of ideas. You certainly have seen that the subject matter has been approached from a pastoral point of view with the aim of presenting not just the text of the classical wedding and funeral services, but a detailed roadmap exploring what a pastor can do with and for people before, during and after these services.

Much of our knowledge and experience in preparing for and conducting these special worship services is dependent upon the examples displayed by pastors with whom we as young ministers have associated along the way. Much of the time, situations fail to provide them with ample opportunities to do an adequate job of teaching us what to do and how to do it. As a local pastor I've spent a good deal of time discussing what to expect with young ministers on the eve of their presiding over their first weddings or funerals. If the truth be known, numbers of well-established pastors don't grow in their knowledge and use of these special services after their classroom days are over. Perhaps you fall into this category and feel the need of some additional support. If so, you hopefully have received the help needed through pondering the contents of this book.

As a theological student, I must have been day dreaming in class when much of this material was presented. I just never gave enough thought as to what it really means to say that weddings and funerals are services of worship. I needed to ask the vital question, "Just exactly what are the essential characteristics of ANY worship service, including weddings and funerals?" It seems to me that one needs to nail down that point before moving on to discuss these special services and to be able to discern how to approach them with more theological integrity.

A good deal of the discussion in Part II about weddings is usually overlooked by writers on this subject. A portion of what has been said here is the result of this author's having been guest participant in several wedding services when it was evident that little pre-planning had been done.

I've suggested something of the content of pre-marital counseling. Perhaps you can use it until your own experience leads you to improve on it.

Included in these pages also is a description of the organization of a wedding rehearsal, and this chapter also furnishes details of the task of the Wedding Director, which deserves your careful consideration. That is in the area of things rarely thought about until the tears of friction start.

In the section on atypical weddings are the descriptions of several situations that may arise without any warning and bearing no clue as to how the minister should handle them. You will now know that someone has been down that path before and has left a pattern which you may follow or from which you may vary.

You will also be aware of the history and meaning of the two major parts of the classical wedding service, which surely leads you to a deeper understanding as to the reasons you do as you will do.

You also hopefully have gained some basis of making the funeral service a more distinctively Christian experience for the families and friends of the deceased. That chapter should give you something with which to compare those practices that you have followed or witnessed.

If some of these things work for you, take them home and call them your own.

In the meantime, blessings on thee and thy house!

W.C.B.